FOCUS ON THE FAMI

EdG

My Truth, Your truth, Whose Truth?

Randy Petersen

TYNDALE

MY TRUTH, YOUR TRUTH, WHOSE TRUTH?

ISBN: 1-56179-868-1

A Focus on the Family book published by Tyndale House Publishers, Wheaton, Illinois.

Editor: John Duckworth
Cover design: Jeff Stoddard

Printed in the United States of America

00 01 02 03 04 05 06/10 9 8 7 6 5 4 3 2 1

Table of Contents

One

The Chat Room

WELCOME TO TEENTALK
Screen Name: wonderboy
Logon 10:49 P.M.

wonderboy: Did you see that some girl's gonna shoot heroin live on the Net?

nobraner: what?

wonderboy: it was on TV. some girl has a webcam and she's going to show herself shooting up

Ynot: So?

wonderboy: She says it's her first time. She's totally clean now, but she wants to start doing drugs.

nobraner: that's so dumb! why would anyone want to start like that?

r2d2: It makes her a star, I guess—a million people watching on her website. Fifteen minutes of fame.

nobraner: people will do anything to be famous

Ynot: So? What's the problem?

Tim4U: Drugs!

Ynot: So?

butterfly: Is that all you can say? So????

Ynot: So, she wants to do drugs. It's a free country.

nobraner: not that free

Ynot: Like you've never smoked pot.

wonderboy: Not me.

r2d2: I did. But I didn't inhale. : o

wonderboy: But heroin. That gets bad.

nobraner: yeah, and it takes over your life

Tim4U: and it's illegal.

r2d2: So is speeding.

Ynot: So what's so bad about this girl doing heroin on her webcam if she wants to?

Tim4U: She's ruining her life. Especially if she never did drugs before. That's a crime.

nobraner: it is a crime. if the cops find her they can put her away for possession

Tim4U: It doesn't matter if she gets caught. It's still illegal.

r2d2: And you've never rolled through a stop sign, or parked in a handicapped spot.

Tim4U: Stop sign, yes. Handicapped spot, no.

nobraner: i think that's the worst . . . parking in a handicapped spot when you're not handicapped.

Ynot: Worse than shooting heroin?

nobraner: i don't know. i just know my grandma is handicapped and sometimes she can't get a space

Ynot: Thanks for sharing. I think they covered that once on Touched by an Angel.

r2d2: I thought we were talking about this heroin chick.

butterfly:	I think it's a fake
Ynot:	But shouldn't she be free to do what she wants?
Tim4U:	Not if she kills herself doing it.
nobraner:	is suicide illegal?
r2d2:	Yeah, you go to jail for the rest of your life. ;)
butterfly:	I don't think it's her first time. I think she's a junkie trying to make a few bucks on a website
Ynot:	So?
Tim4U:	Then she's cheating the public, and that's wrong.
nobraner:	anybody who wants to watch someone shoot heroin deserves to be cheated
r2d2:	I'll just rent Trainspotting.
butterfly:	I saw that movie. Good music, but boring.
r2d2:	Thank you, Roger Ebert.
Ynot:	So, I still want to know what makes heroin worse than pot.
Tim4U:	It's all bad. You shouldn't do any drugs.
nobraner:	and she's going to get other people doing it, too. that's what happens when you give publicity to something
Ynot:	But don't they have a free choice, too?
butterfly:	People are stupid. They'll jump off a building if they see someone on TV doing it
Ynot:	I'm just saying we can't tell people how to live their lives.
Tim4U:	But drugs are wrong!
Ynot:	So you paid attention in health class. But what's so bad about drugs?
Tim4U:	They're just wrong! Don't you care about morality?

Ynot:	What makes you the authority? You've got your morality, I've got mine. Whatever floats your boat.
Tim4U:	Some things are just wrong!
Ynot:	Why? Because your mommy told you so?
Tim4U:	No, because they are. Can anyone help me out here?
wonderboy:	Not me.
butterfly:	no clue
Ynot:	Look, who is this girl hurting when she shoots up on the Net?
nobraner:	herself
Ynot:	Maybe that's right FOR HER. Shouldn't she have freedom over her own body?
Tim4U:	Some choices are bad for us.
Ynot:	says who? Look, Tim4U, you don't have to do it. Maybe that choice is bad FOR YOU but why should you keep this girl from doing it?
Tim4U:	I'm not making my point very well, I guess. Can't somebody help me out?
butterfly:	Not me
nobraner:	i agree with you, i just don't know why
wonderboy:	Sorry.

REAL LIFE
Home of Greg (aka wonderboy)
Next Morning

"I heard you up late last night. Homework again?"
Greg's mom was putting away the breakfast cereal as her

son stuffed a soup spoon of Quaker Life into his mouth. "Mmmm-hmmmm," he replied—which really wasn't a lie, he figured, because lies require *words* and these were just unintelligible sounds. If his mother interpreted these sounds to mean that he was indeed working on homework until midnight, rather than surfing the Net—well, that was her problem. Truth didn't have to be an issue, did it?

After all, Greg generally managed to stay afloat at school, even if he didn't spend much time on homework. He had his ways of navigating the system. That was what mattered—what *worked*, not just what was true.

"Oh, Mom, is it okay if I stay over at Brian's tonight? It's Friday."

"Are Brian's parents going to be home?"

"Sure. We were just gonna go up to see his brother's basketball game at college, so we'd be kinda late anyway. It's probably easier if I just sack out there."

Greg knew his mom was studying his face, searching for any crack of deceit. There had been a party at Brian's the year before, when his parents were away, and some kids had gotten seriously drunk—like emergency-room drunk. That made the whole event rather public, and Greg had been grounded for two weeks.

That made telling the whole truth about tonight seem rather unwise. The facts: After the game there was going to be a big party at the college Brian's brother attended. Greg and Brian were planning to crash it. If all went well, they'd be back to Brian's at 5:00 or 6:00 A.M. Everything he'd told his mom was true; he'd just failed to mention the party. So, as she scanned his face with her lie-detector eyes, Greg was a rock.

"I guess that'll be okay," she finally said.

"Love ya, Mom," said Greg, lurching from his chair, grazing her cheek, and grabbing his books in one motion. Then he was out the door to catch the school bus.

Amanda was already on the bus, as usual, in the back seat. Greg made his way back there and gave her the same kind of kiss he'd just given his mother. He saved the more passionate kisses for private moments with Amanda.

Everyone said they looked great together. About five inches shorter, she fit right under his arm. They both had dark hair and brown eyes and slender builds. A match made in heaven, people said.

He might have agreed—a month ago. But lately he'd found himself just going through the motions. He didn't want to hurt Amanda by breaking up with her. But he couldn't bring himself to tell her the truth, either—that she was, well, kind of boring.

Should he be a selfish jerk and dump her? Or stay with her and continue this loveless masquerade? He'd decided to try the latter, to try to ease out of the relationship slowly. He didn't think it was working.

And then there was Chrissy—a cute girl on the yearbook staff who seemed interested in him. He couldn't really *date* her until he resolved things with Amanda, but he could plan for the future, couldn't he?

"You wanna go to a movie tonight?" Amanda was asking.

"I can't," Greg replied. "I told you, Brian and I are going up to see Billy play."

"Can I come, too?"

Uh-oh. This is not part of the plan. Do I tell the truth, or—
Or not.

"Look, Amanda," he said, taking her hands in his, "you and I are going out tomorrow night. We'll have a great time. Tonight it's kind of a guy thing, okay?"

Her brown eyes fluttered with disappointment. "Okay," she said finally.

Greg couldn't breathe a sigh of relief, but he wanted to. The truth was that Chrissy happened to have a friend at the same college, and Greg had offered her a ride. It wasn't really a *date*, but they'd have a chance to get to know each other. *Maybe Chrissy will even come to the party . . .*

But as the bus rumbled toward school, a thought kept bothering him. *Do I really know what's right anymore?* He remembered the chat room last night, with everyone talking about the girl shooting heroin. It was all verbal Ping-Pong, with nobody sounding sure of anything. That one guy, Tim something, seemed to have an idea—but he wasn't convincing anyone.

But what if that other character—"Ynot"—was right? What if something could be true "for me" or true "for you"? Wasn't that the way people lived nowadays?

If truth was in the eye of the beholder, he could lie to his mom, mess around with Amanda, and see Chrissy on the side—because it would be right FOR GREG.

That would make life so much easier, he thought.

In homeroom, Greg handed Brian a photocopy of his math homework. "Remember to change two or three of the answers. Do you have the history stuff?"

"Oh, no," Brian gasped. "I completely forgot. I got out of

history yesterday to meet with the guidance counselor. I never got the assignment. Sorry, man."

"That's okay," Greg said. "I've got a study hall third period. I guess I'll do it then. But you're buying all my refreshments at the game tonight."

They'd started this racket a few months earlier, trading geometry assignments for history. Since they were willing to fudge a few answers, the teachers hadn't caught on.

But when third period came around, Greg sat in the library, staring at the history assignment Brian had failed to do for him. "How do they expect me to find this stuff?" he moaned.

He looked around. There, at the other end of the table, was geeky little Frankie Cheever. Greg didn't want to be seen talking to him, but these were desperate times.

"Hey, Frankie. You know any websites about the Korean War?"

Startled, Frankie looked up through his thick glasses. "Are you . . . talking to me?"

"It's this Twentieth Century History course. I've got to find out about the Korean War by next period."

Frankie seemed glad for any chance to make a human connection. "Let me see," he said, coming over to sit next to Greg. "Here's a great search engine that could help you." He wrote a Web address on a slip of paper. "You can try that computer over there."

Just then, out of the corner of his eye, Greg saw three kids walk into the library—some of the smart kids of the school, the social kids, people it was good to know.

Uh-oh, he thought.

"What's this? You're hanging out with Frankie now?"

teased Jason, the yearbook's photo editor. "Or did they finally put you in special ed?" The others laughed and Greg blushed.

This is obviously no time to tell the truth, Greg thought.

"Hey, he sat down at my table," Greg stammered, getting up and not looking back. "What could I do? It's a free country."

Jason snickered, then moved on. Greg headed for the computer, not wanting to be seen thanking Frankie—or to look the outcast in the eye.

Greg never did finish the assignment. But his sob story to the teacher seemed plausible enough. "I got halfway through it last night and my stupid computer crashed." The teacher bought it.

Yeah, Greg thought. *The truth just complicates things.*

After school, Greg headed for Chrissy's locker. He spotted her way down the hallway, her short, blond hair shining, her smile radiating. "We can pick you up at five," he told her. "The game's at seven and it's an hour up there. Maybe we can grab a bite to eat."

"That would be nice," she said. "Do you know where I live?"

"Sure," he answered. "See you at five—"

Suddenly Amanda came walking out of the next classroom. "Greg!" she said. "What are you doing at this end of the building?"

"Just, uh, some yearbook business." He grabbed her arm and moved her down the hallway, away from Chrissy. "Setting up a meeting."

"For five o'clock?"

"Yeah, people's schedules are so crazy these days." Hey, he wasn't really telling an untruth. This was *his* truth. People's schedules *were* crazy. He *was* setting up a meeting with Chrissy. He just didn't want Amanda to know what *kind* of meeting.

Amanda gave Greg a quick kiss and hurried off to drama practice. Greg turned—and saw Chrissy standing ten feet away.

"Are you and Amanda still together?" she asked.

Greg swallowed. What version of the truth should he try this time?

"Well," he drawled, "yes and no."

Brilliant, Sherlock! He groaned to himself.

"But I thought you said—"

"It's kind of complicated, Chrissy."

"So maybe I shouldn't go tonight."

"No, Chrissy, it's all right. We're just giving you a ride."

"I don't feel right about it," she said.

He sagged, listening to her footsteps *clack-clack* down the barren hallway.

Yeah, he thought. *Truth just complicates things.*

Almost as much as lies.

Walking home that day, he couldn't help wondering whether somehow, somewhere, there was a better way to live.

AND NOW, BACK TO YOU . . .

What does all this have to do with you?

Like Greg, you probably can't go very far through a day without facing a question about what's true—and what isn't. What's right? What's wrong? How do you know?

Greg isn't such a bad guy. You probably know him—or someone like him. He tries to be truthful most of the time, and he makes sure every lie has a little truth in it. He doesn't want to hurt his girlfriend, but he doesn't want to limit his options, either. He'll cheat on an assignment, but tells himself that it's mainly to help a friend.

And so he muddles through life, getting himself in jams and trying to get himself out. He's no different from most people today. They're shifting on the fly, making up the rules as they go along. Their ideas about truth rest on a flimsy web of feelings and opinions.

Sometimes it seems as if the whole planet is like that chat room. Some of us have a vague feeling about truth, about right and wrong—but we have no clue *why*. Whenever someone dares to express a firm opinion, he or she is hooted down as "narrow-minded" or "judgmental."

The only rule, it seems, is that there are no rules. The only thing people seem to know for sure is that you can't know anything for sure.

"Every idea is as valuable as any other idea, whether it makes sense or not," a kid in your Modern Problems class may say. "Something may be true *for you*, but not for me," says another. Are they right? Who decides?

You see it on those daytime TV talk shows, too. You know, the ones that tackle topics like "My Mom Stole My Boyfriend." Those shows are all about right and wrong. Most of the people on stage feel they've been wronged in some way, and they're trying to make things right—maybe by throwing a chair at somebody. Everyone in the audience has an opinion: "You're a loser! Get rid of him! Why are you still living with that jerk?"

But nobody seems to know what the *truth* is.

That doesn't make life simpler. As Greg found, it makes life a lot more complicated.

You may be wondering, along with "wonderboy": Can't we find a better way to live?

The answer is yes.

It's going to take a little looking to find it, but the search is worth it.

If you want the truth, let's get started.

Two

Search Engine

WELCOME TO TEENTALK
Screen Name: nobraner
Logon 7:03 P.M.

butterfly:	Hey, nb, how's trix?
nobraner:	don't ask
butterfly:	bad day, huh?
Tim4U:	What's wrong?
nobraner:	nothing
Tim4U:	Come on! You can tell us. We're just a handful of your closest personal e-mates.
nobraner:	it's nothing
r2d2:	That's the cool thing about the Net. No one knows who you really are, so you can say ANYTHING.
butterfly:	nobraner doesn't want to talk about it, OK? But if you do, nb, we're here for you.
r2d2:	At least until that X-Files repeat comes on. Then I'm outta here.
wonderboy:	I'm stuck here. My mom grounded me.
r2d2:	Poor baby

butterfly: What'd you do?

wonderboy: Just some lies I told her. Sneaking out.

butterfly: But you still have us.

[Hulkster has entered the chat room.]

wonderboy: Where've you been?

Hulkster: Lifting weights, mostly. Coach says I'll lose my starting spot on the football team if I don't bulk up.

butterfly: Bummer

Hulkster: Yeah, I'm pretty depressed about it.

r2d2: Look, nobraner, another downer in our midst.

butterfly: You still there, nb?

nobraner: yeah

Hulkster: What's wrong with nb?

nobraner: NOTHING IS WRONG

Hulkster: Sorry I asked.

nobraner: no, that's exactly it. nothing is what's wrong. i am nothing. my life is nothing. there is nothing important that i do

r2d2: Well, isn't that something?

butterfly: Shut up

Tim4U: It can't be that bad, can it?

butterfly: Yeah, there has to be something in your life, something you enjoy.

nobraner: not right now. nothing that's worth anything. give me one good reason for living. one thing that provides meaning for your life.

r2d2: Peanut butter.

butterfly:	Go watch your aliens.
r2d2:	Maybe I will.
	[r2d2 has left the chat room.]
wonderboy:	My mom always says to leave the world in better shape than you found it.
nobraner:	why?
wonderboy:	Beats me.
butterfly:	I think life has meaning if you feel good about yourself
nobraner:	and if you don't?
Tim4U:	Helping others is a good thing.
nobraner:	helping them do what? Live meaningless lives? Isn't the whole thing kind of circular? i just don't see any point to it.
Hulkster:	Look, you're down right now. But maybe tomorrow you'll feel better. I think you gotta just grab for the gusto.
nobraner:	and what exactly will gusto do for me?
butterfly:	It will help you feel good about yourself.
nobraner:	I DON'T WANT TO FEEL GOOD ABOUT MYSELF. I WANT TO KNOW WHY I'M HERE.
Tim4U:	We're trying to help you figure that out.
nobraner:	sorry, it's not working.
Tim4U:	Maybe if you found something to believe in.
	[nobraner has left the chat room.]
Hulkster:	Elvis has left the building.
butterfly:	I hope she's OK
wonderboy:	So, Hulkster, what's going on with the Dallas Cowboys?

REAL LIFE
In the Room of Julie (aka nobraner)
Next Day, After School

"What's blathering?"

"What?"

"Blathering. It's there on page 42: 'Yesterday evening we spent blathering about nothing in particular.'"

"Oh." Julie was teamed with her friend Sheri on a lit project. This was probably the eightieth question Sheri had asked this afternoon, as they sat in Julie's bedroom preparing for a class presentation. "I suppose it means talking. Just talking with no special purpose in mind."

"I get it!" Sheri bubbled. "Like what *we* do most of the time."

That's exactly the problem, Julie thought. There was no purpose to their talking, no purpose to anything they did—including this Twentieth Century Literature class.

"I don't like this Samuel Beckett guy," Sheri said. "He seems pretty strange."

"*Very* strange," Julie sighed, twisting her well-thumbed copy of *Waiting for Godot*. "But this strange guy, with his strange play, is the one we have to tell the class about. How are we going to do that?"

Sheri absently twirled her thick, black curls. "I wish we could take Twenty-*first* Century Literature. There's less of that."

"True." Julie lay on her bed and stared at the ceiling. "Have you noticed how few of the writers we've been studying seem—I don't know—*happy*? No, that's not the word." She scoured her brain, trying to name the problem she'd been having—not only with this class, but with her whole life. "I don't know. It's like they're good writers, but some of them just don't seem to *care*."

"Like they're blathering," Sheri suggested.

"Maybe that's it. Like this play: It's just two guys talking, waiting for someone who never shows up. Two more guys come, they say stuff you can't figure out, and they leave. And the first two guys talk some more. There's your book report."

"It's like nothing happens."

"Exactly. Nothing."

It was the word Julie had been searching for. *Nothing*. It had haunted her for weeks, even months. At first she'd thought it was just a bad mood. But it lasted day after day after day.

Nothing was wrong with her. She dreamed about *nothing*, wanted *nothing*, lived for *nothing*. She started each day knowing that *nothing* awaited her, and she went to sleep knowing *nothing* had happened.

Julie flung her copy of *Waiting for Godot* hard against her bed. "I mean, it's just so pointless!"

Sheri seemed stunned by the sudden emotion. She searched Julie's face for some clue: Was she joking or not? Then, in her little-girl voice, she suggested, "Isn't that, like, the point?"

An hour later, after Sheri left, Julie went for a walk to clear her head. Or maybe to find something to put *into* her head, pushing away the *nothing* that had been growing there.

What's it all about? Why should I even bother getting up in the morning? How can I get through the day?

She thought of her dad. He seemed to find meaning in following the Almighty Dollar. She never saw him more happy than when he was online, searching for new stocks to invest in—or more upset than when one of those stocks went south. Was greed the way to go?

Not if the rich kids at school were any indication, she thought. They had everything money could buy, but they were the neediest people she knew. She didn't want to be like them. *They* didn't want to be like them. No, money wasn't the answer. It was just more *nothing*, tinted green.

What about Mom? She was a marvel, a secretary who got a business degree later in life and started her climb up the ladder. Mom clearly had something to prove, and she was proving it every day at work.

So was that the answer? Success? But what *was* success? Pushing new stacks of paper around a larger desk?

Big brother James didn't seem to have the answer, either. He was in college, majoring in parties. His goals in life were to consume as much alcohol as possible, to listen to loud music at all times, and to have sex with every girl on campus. Maybe that was a way to chase away the *nothing* in your soul—get all the kicks you can, as fast as you can. But when he'd come home last Christmas, James had been a blob, living in a constant haze. She didn't want to be like that.

She thought about the chat room. Her e-friends had tried to help, but it was all rather pitiful:

"Feel good about yourself." *If you're depressed, get a makeover! Right.*

"Leave this world in better shape than you found it."

That's sweet, but why? Who cares what shape the world's in after I'm gone?

"Help others." Sure, her favorite people were those who tried to be helpful. But wasn't that just another attempt to rearrange the furniture on the *Titanic*?

All the options seemed to miss the point—if there was a point. They were feeble attempts to make things better, to drown out the nagging questions, to entertain people as they sank into the swamp of life's meaninglessness.

Isn't there anything I can hold onto? Julie thought. *A reason to live, not just an excuse?*

She had circled the block. As dusk shrouded the horizon, she walked to the door and re-entered her empty house.

AND NOW, BACK TO YOU . . .

What on earth are you doing?

Let me put that another way: *What are you doing on earth?*

Why are you here? Is there a purpose to your life, or are you just floating along until you die?

We all want a reason to live, don't we? It seems we're wired that way. Fish gotta swim, birds gotta fly, and we gotta . . . what?

Ten different people may finish that sentence twenty different ways, but they all seem to need a purpose. Without a sense of direction, we get depressed—like Julie.

It's no use saying, "Cheer up! It's not so bad!" The problem has nothing to do with things being *bad*. Things could be bad or good—but without any purpose in life, things don't really *matter.* Why should you get up in the morning and brush your teeth and sit in your history class and chow down the mystery meat in the school cafeteria? What's the point?

Exhibit A: Scott is 16 and madly in love with his first-ever girlfriend. For three months he focuses entirely on her. Then she dumps him. He lies in bed for three days, telling his mom he's got the flu—but he really just lacks the energy to do anything. His reason for being—that girlfriend—has been taken away. His life seems to have no meaning anymore.

We want something deeper to keep us going. As Dr. Doug Geivett, Biola University philosophy professor, says, we need "a sense of being worthy of the life each of us has, and of…human value, dignity." Otherwise, we just languish with this terminal disease called life, waiting to die. Tragically, some kids choose to hasten the process of that "terminal disease"—committing suicide because they no longer see the point of living.

As for Scott, maybe he'll get back on his feet and find some other purpose for living—another girl, basketball, his CD collection, volunteering in a soup kitchen. But his next romance could crash and burn. An injury may keep him off the basketball team. Eventually he'll be selling his Smashmouth CDs at a yard sale. And even the soup kitchen may seem old hat before long.

These life-purposes we grab for are really substitutes for some *ultimate* purpose.

But what is it?

To start figuring this out, pretend you're an actor. You've been hired to portray a character in a movie; to get ready for a scene, you need to understand the character's motivation. So you ask yourself, *Where is this character coming from? Where is he or she going?* Is the character coming from a steam bath or a snowstorm? Is he or she going to an all-you-can-eat buffet or a firing squad?

If we want to understand our own motivation, our purpose in life, we need to ask those questions about ourselves, too. Where are *we* coming from? Where are *we* going?

Some have decided that we've "come from" a bowl of soup. You probably already know the basics of the evolutionary story: A "primordial soup" spawned amino acids and proteins, the building blocks of life. Then came amoebas and amphibians and apes and finally us—pretty much by accident.

If we've come from soup, by chance, we're just a collection of cells. When we "fall in love," it's just a chemical process that evolved to advance the species. Things like "kindness" and "having a soul" are just ideas that evolved for the same reason.

According to this view, where are we *going*? What's our ultimate purpose? Random evolution gives us two: *survival* and *serving nature.*

If you've been paying attention in science class, you've heard of "survival of the fittest." In this scheme, it's your goal to be the brightest, biggest, and most beautiful. If you're a loser—well, tough.

You say surviving isn't enough for you? No problem! The evolutionary process suggests that you can *serve nature*, too. Since "nature" has shepherded you through all those mutations, you need to honor it. That includes *your* nature. Be who you are! If you feel like doing something, do it! It's only natural!

In this view there's no bottom-line truth, no wrong except squelching what comes naturally (unless it pollutes the nature around us). Just try to have the best time you can—and if you die with the most toys, you win.

Where does that leave us? Fighting, for one thing. My

nature collides with yours when we're both grabbing for the same stuff. A few people win; everyone else loses. And as Julie found, even those who "win" end up living lives that mean . . . nothing.

So, is there a better way?

Some say there is. It's an ultimate purpose that seems to come out of nowhere. They say it's buried deep inside us like a Ken Griffey, Jr. rookie card forgotten under a stack of old report cards in your attic.

That purpose is *love.*

They're not talking about goo-goo eyes in study hall, but about wanting to put someone else first. If everyone did that, the world would be a better place, wouldn't it?

Unfortunately, it's very hard to do. We may try to do the right thing, but we keep coming back to a certain selfishness that seems ingrained in us. Love may be a great purpose, but it's awfully hard to stay on track—without help from someone or something more powerful than we are.

But that's exactly what these people believe—that there *is* a personal being of great power who created us. That's how they answer the "Where did we come from?" question. They believe this Creator, God, designed us. And just as a motorcycle or a DVD player or a fork is designed for a purpose, so we have a purpose: *to serve the Creator.*

They don't see serving Him as a big burden, either. They believe He invented love, and wants a loving relationship with us. They believe growing closer to Him is the answer to the "Where are we going?" question.

In a world of so much nothing, isn't that something worth looking into—especially if it can get you through the day?

Who knows? It might even be a place to find . . . the truth.

Three

Emoticons

WELCOME TO TEENTALK
Screen Name: Hulkster
Logon 8:17 P.M.

butterfly:	I need some help from you guys.
Tim4U:	Shoot.
nobraner:	girls too, or just guys?
butterfly:	Everybody! HEEELLLPPPPP! (:> 0)
Tim4U:	What seems to be the problem?
butterfly:	Boys.
nobraner:	uh-oh
butterfly:	Two boys in particular. The first we'll call Jared.
Hulkster:	What's his real name?
butterfly:	Jared.
Hulkster:	Oh.
butterfly:	We've been going out for a year now. I really love Jared and he loves me.
Hulkster:	That's a real problem.
butterfly:	No. I even said I would marry him after we graduate

Hulkster:	Now THAT'S a problem!
butterfly:	No, the problem is Carlos.
nobraner:	uh-oh
butterfly:	I think I'm in love with Carlos.
nobraner:	who's carlos???
butterfly:	Jared's neighbor.
nobraner:	uh-oh
butterfly:	I went there once looking for Jared and he wasn't there so I started talking to Carlos.
Hulkster:	Next door to Jared's house?
butterfly:	it's a row house.
Tim4U:	Does Jared know?
butterfly:	Not yet, I think.
nobraner:	he will
butterfly:	I don't want to hurt Jared. I still want to marry him.
Tim4U:	You're kidding.
butterfly:	No, I told you. I really love Jared. He's a good guy. I feel good when I'm with him. But I'm in love with Carlos. When I'm with him I see colors.
Hulkster:	Dump em both.
Tim4U:	What would Jared do if he knew about Carlos?
butterfly:	He'd be mad.
Hulkster:	Dump em both.
Tim4U:	Is that all you can say, hulk?
Hulkster:	It's just so stupid! You girls are totally driven by your feelings!
nobraner:	and guys aren't???
Hulkster:	Not as much. Butterfly, don't you ever THINK about these relationships?

butterfly:	Sure I do.
Hulkster:	Then why do you get into them? Is either Jared or Carlos GOOD FOR YOU??
butterfly:	They make me feel good . . . in different ways.
Hulkster:	See what I mean?
nobraner:	guys go by feelings too
Hulkster:	I don't. Feelings get you in trouble. You got to look at a situation, choose the best way, and go there. Don't follow your feelings.
nobraner:	Thank you, Mr. ANDROID
Hulkster:	You've got to admit that Butterfly would be better off right now if she didn't follow her feelings.
butterfly:	But I still don't know what to do.
Hulkster:	Dump em both.

REAL LIFE
Outside the Locker Room of Mike (aka Hulkster)
Next Day

"No, Mike. I just don't feel right about it." Jonica had assumed a tone of voice that slammed the door on a future discussion.

"You girls and your feelings," Mike muttered.

"What?"

Mike looked his girlfriend in the eye and forced a smile. "Oh, nothing," he said sweetly.

So it was off, the weekend trip. He wanted to talk about it some more, but there was a meeting of the football squad. They said a strained good-bye with a quick, dutiful kiss.

Girls and their feelings, Mike thought as he headed for the gym. *Can't she see this is perfect for us?*

She was like that girl in the chat room last night, letting her feelings float between two different guys. Both of the guys were probably losers. If she was smart, she'd dump them both, but girls tended to follow their feelings. He remembered something from science class about how females were wired to be more emotional, like in their brains and hormones and stuff. *I'm glad guys don't have that problem.*

The coach lectured them about commitment, about how football had to be their number one priority. They had to eat, sleep, and breathe football. Hulk wondered how Jonica would feel if she heard that.

Coach had a way of working the team into a frenzy. Soon they were all shouting together, voicing their total commitment. Hulk looked around the circle and saw his buddies Raider and Frog and Allen and Whitey, guys he would throw down his body for, guys he would die for.

There were some new guys in the room, too, including one giant who'd just moved to the city from the suburbs. He was introduced as Raymond, a middle linebacker. This guy had an inch or two of height on Hulk and was a bit broader. He also had arms that looked like legs. Now he'd be competing for Hulk's position.

"Probably slow as peanut butter," whispered Raider. "No one's faster off the ball than you, Hulkster."

Still, Hulk was worried. Even more so after the meeting, when Coach called him into his office.

"You're a good player, Hulk, but we can't afford to sit on our laurels," Coach said. "We need 200 percent from every man on this team. Are you committed to this program, Hulk?"

"You know I am, Coach."

"Maybe you met Raymond out there. This kid can help us a lot, I think. He's going to get an even chance to win that middle linebacker spot. I like you, Hulk, but I can't afford to play favorites. You have to be ready to do whatever it takes to win that job."

"Yes, sir."

"Whatever it takes," the coach repeated, with that squint that said he meant business. "Do you understand me?"

"Whatever it takes," Mike echoed.

He swallowed, his throat tight. *This is the thanks I get for busting my rear for three years on this team. What if I don't win my position back? I can't sit on the bench, not in my senior year. What will people think?*

As Mike left the office, Scout tagged along. Scout was the equipment manager for the team, a guy who'd been a third-stringer ten years ago and basically had no life. Now he collected the practice footballs, gathered the towels—and performed a few other services.

"Got your work cut out for you, huh?" Scout chirped.

"Yeah," Mike moaned. "How am I gonna beat that guy?"

Scout's squeaky voice was annoyingly cheerful. "He's big."

"I could lift weights every day for three years and still not have arms like his."

"Maybe you could," Scout suggested. "With a little help."

"There's no way," Mike insisted. "Thanks, but—oh, you mean *help.*"

He's talking about steroids, doofus, Mike told himself. He knew those illegal drugs could bulk a guy up fast, but also mess with his mind and body. He also knew that a couple of guys on the team used steroids, but it was all very hush-hush. Guys didn't want other guys to know they needed chemical crutches. They pretended their new muscles came from weightlifting.

"Everybody needs a little help now and then," Scout was saying. "Nothing wrong with that. I mean, if you're really committed to the team and all, you'll do whatever it takes, right? Whatever it takes."

Scout had turned into this weird little chipmunk, a sur-real windup toy. He just kept pushing. "No one has to know. I know this guy, see, he gets it for me. No questions asked. I can have the juice here tomorrow. You say the word, Hulk, and it's yours. Just pump in the magic juice and you're the *Incredible* Hulk, man. Nothing to worry about."

"Tomorrow?"

"Twenty-four hours, man. Right here. Same bat time, same bat channel."

This would be a lot more tempting if Scout wasn't so creepy. Still, it was tempting enough. Scout was the channel through which Hulk's future flowed. Juice or no juice? What would it be?

"I'll meet you here tomorrow, Scout. But no promises. I have to think about it."

"Sure thing," Scout chirped, and slithered into the weight room.

Walking home, Hulk weighed his options. Stay clean and maybe lose his starting spot to something named Raymond. Take the drugs and risk those hormonal changes and liver damage and sterility he'd read about. Not to mention that steroids could make guys a little crazy, even violent.

He wanted to talk with Jonica about it, but he knew she

wouldn't understand. She'd say she didn't "feel right" about it, and that would be the end of that. He was trying to deal with the *facts* of the matter. Feelings had nothing to do with it.

He frowned. After all he'd done for the team, how dare Coach question his commitment? He was more committed than anyone! He'd show them!

Whatever it takes? I'll do it.

"What's wrong, baby?" cooed Jonica on the phone that night. She heard the tension in his voice from the first hello.

"Nothing," Mike answered. "You wouldn't understand."

AND NOW, BACK TO YOU . . .

You're taking a math test.

It's pretty challenging, but you've studied hard and you know how to do these equations. Question 1 gives you a bunch of numbers and letters and asks you to "solve for x." You start to work out the problem, but then you get a feeling. The answer *feels* like a 3.

So you boldly write your answer on the test paper: $x=3$.

Question 2 *feels* like a 5. Question 3 *feels* like $x=13y$. No need to mess with multiplication or division; you're *feeling* it. You're in the zone!

You're polishing off the twentieth question while others are still breaking down the first. Proudly you place your completed paper on the desk of your surprised teacher.

And how will you *feel* when you get the test back with a big, red zero?

Feelings are fine, but they're no way to do algebra. At

some point they have to give way to something more solid.

Still, many people today live by their feelings. In a million TV commercials, pop songs, and billboards we're told to go by our gut. "Can't fight the feeling." "Feel the power." In other words, follow your feelings. Do what feels right.

Feelings aren't bad. Sometimes they can help you sort through a confusing situation. But in life as in algebra, you can't always trust them to steer you toward truth.

Take the case of "butterfly" from the chat room. She felt "good" with Jared and Carlos—and made decisions on that basis. But now she feels confused and guilty.

And how about Mike? He thought Jonica and girls in general were too emotional, but his decision to use steroids was based on feelings. Faced with the prospect of losing his starting spot, he was angry and afraid. Those feelings were propelling him toward a disastrous choice.

According to the lyrics of one old song, "It can't be wrong if it feels so right." But is that true? If you feel like having sex, should you? What if you feel like robbing a bank? Or blowing up the state capitol building?

Is it possible that some feelings are better than others, because they're based on something more solid? Can it be that some feelings help us live better lives—while others encourage us to destroy our lives?

Let's take food as an example. Say you like Taco Bell Chalupas. So you eat 20 or 30 of them every day—because you feel like it. No problem, right? Wrong. As your bathroom scale tips 400 pounds, you begin to realize that too much of a good thing is a bad thing.

"No fair," you might say. "I should be able to follow my feelings about chalupas. I shouldn't have to listen to all those narrow-minded 'health experts' with their 'objective' rules about calories and food groups."

You don't have to listen. But you do have to live with the results of following your feelings—which could include anything from limited wardrobe choices to death from obesity.

So if feelings don't always lead us to truth, what does? Is there a better way?

There may be—*if* we've been fashioned by a Creator who wants a relationship with us. In that case, our feelings would be gifts to us. They wouldn't be the authority, though. Our Creator probably would reserve that role for Himself.

How do you feel about that?

Four

Online Poll

WELCOME TO TEENTALK
Screen Name: butterfly
Logon 6:59 P.M.

butterfly:	Howdy, friend. How are you?
nobraner:	depressed, as usual
wonderboy:	What else is new?
nobraner:	but enough about me. how are you? any weekend plans?
r2d2:	Nothing.
nobraner:	you really need to get a life
r2d2:	Had one. Hated it. Got back online.
nobraner:	sounds like my life
butterfly:	Speaking of life, what's everyone else doing this weekend?
Hulkster:	Lifting weights.
r2d2:	Very large cans of Mountain Dew?
Hulkster:	No, weights. I have to build my strength for football.
nobraner:	i hear wonder bread builds strong bodies 12 ways.

33

Hulkster: Thanks, but I'm trying to avoid artificial sub-
stances.

r2d2: So, Timfarooni, what are you doing this
weekend?

Tim4U: Not much. The church youth group is going
bowling and then out for pizza.

r2d2: Oooh. Too much excitement for me.

butterfly: Moving right along . . . Wonderboy, what are
you doing?

wonderboy: Writing a paper.

r2d2: Sounds fun. Can I come, too?

[Ynot has entered the chat room.]

Ynot: Hey there, fiends.

butterfly: Welcome back. Long time no "e."

Ynot: What's the topic tonight?

butterfly: The weekend.

Tim4U: Why do teachers think that a long weekend
means extra time for homework?

butterfly: Like we don't have anything better to do.

Hulkster: What's your topic on the paper?

wonderboy: I don't know.

Hulkster: You ARE in trouble.

r2d2: Choose something you already know so you
can fudge it.

wonderboy: What do you mean by fudge?

r2d2: Make up resources if you can't find them. If
you do it right you can impress your
teacher.

wonderboy: How?

r2d2: By making up really cool books that the
teacher can't find.

Ynot:	Danger, Will Robinson!
r2d2:	No one will ever know they're a figment of your imagination.
Ynot:	Danger! Danger!
butterfly:	Who's Will Robinson?
r2d2:	What's so dangerous?
Ynot:	Thanks to amazon.com and barnes&noble a teacher can check any book you cite. I have a better idea.
wonderboy:	What?
Ynot:	Buy the whole thing.
wonderboy:	Huh?
Ynot:	Buy the paper. Smarter people than you have gone before and they will sell you their handi-work.
wonderboy:	But then it's not my paper.
Ynot:	Bingo was his name-o.
wonderboy:	How much?
butterfly:	Bingo was whose name-o?
Ynot:	That depends.
butterfly:	On what?
Ynot:	On length, subject, number of footnotes, college or high school.
wonderboy:	I don't think I can do this.
r2d2:	How much would it be?
Ynot:	You could probably get a C for fifty bucks, get an A or B for a hundred.
butterfly:	That's a lot!
Ynot:	How much is your weekend worth to you?
nobraner:	mine? about a buck.
Ynot:	You pay by credit card, they e-mail you the

	text, you dress it up a bit to make it look like yours, you print it out and hand it in. No one ever knows.
wonderboy:	I don't think I could do that.
Ynot:	Y Not?
Tim4U:	It's not right. It's not his paper. What is he learning from that?
Ynot:	He's learning how to beat the system.
r2d2:	And really, how much are you going to learn by copying from the encyclopedia? It's the same thing.
Tim4U:	It's not, it's cheating!
Ynot:	Everyone does it.
Tim4U:	Not everyone. Not me.
wonderboy:	What do you other guys think? I'm like in-between on this. Let's just take a vote. What do you think I should do?
r2d2:	Sounds like a plan. I'm for buying the paper online.
Tim4U:	I'm not. Don't do it.
nobraner:	it's stupid. i say no.
Hulkster:	Honestly, I think I would buy it. I mean, what difference does it make? When have you ever learned anything by writing a paper?
Ynot:	And you know what I think. That's three for buying the paper and two against. Has every-one voted?
butterfly:	Not me. But I can't decide. I just don't know.
Ynot:	Then it's 3-2 with one abstention. Let me get you that ordering info.

REAL LIFE
Home of Maria (aka butterfly)
Next Morning

Maria slept in on Saturday. Eight o'clock.

In her dream she'd been running for president and was very worried that she didn't have the right outfit for her acceptance speech. She was just deciding on the ripped blue jeans, which matched her fingernail polish, when she woke up.

Her five-year-old twin brothers were having a little too much fun in the hallway. She pulled a blanket over her head, but it didn't help. Saturday had begun.

Soon she was dancing around the kitchen, making pancakes for the boys and for her two sisters. The oldest, Sara, tried to help but usually got in the way. She was only ten.

"More butter, Sara, the pan's nearly dry. . . . Where do you think? In the refrigerator. . . . On the door. . . . On the shelf in the door. . . . Behind that little flap thing. . . . Right in front of you! . . . Never mind, I'll get it."

Sara has a sweet smile, Maria thought, *but she's dumb as a post. The curse of the Gonzalez women—all beauty, no brains.*

But Maria was trying to change that. She worked hard at school, very hard. It didn't come easily, but she was pulling a B average.

She also had to help her mother run the house. Mama worked a late shift, so Maria had to get the kids up and ready each morning. She could relax a little in the afternoon, usually hanging out with her boyfriend Jared. After she put the kids to bed at night she went into her room and sat down at the computer.

It was her pride and joy, an old 486 Compaq she'd bought

secondhand from Jared's cousin with her own babysitting money. After hooking up a 56K modem she was online, doing research for school and occasionally stopping by her favorite chat room. She felt free when she chatted on the Internet. It was like touring the world. There were people from all over the country in that chat room. She could flutter anywhere she wanted, which is why she'd chosen the screen name "butterfly."

Last night's conversation had stayed with her. "Wonderboy" hadn't been sure whether to buy a term paper rather than writing it himself. He'd let the group decide, and "butterfly" had refused to cast a vote.

She still couldn't figure out where to stand on the issue. Would it be wrong to hand in a paper you hadn't written? She wouldn't do it herself, but if everyone else said it was okay, who was she to disagree? Besides, who had cast the "no" votes? The church guy, Tim, who was probably used to telling people what to do, and the "nobraner" girl who was so depressed she'd vote no on blowing up an asteroid that was headed for earth.

It's not my battle, Maria thought.

But it was. She had a paper of her own due in another week, for Modern European History. She was planning to start work on it this weekend if Carlos didn't call. The thought of buying a history paper fluttered through her mind, but she didn't have the money. Besides, that wouldn't be Maria. She *worked* for what she got.

Carlos didn't call. So Saturday afternoon, after her chores were finished, she sat down at her 486 to surf the world on the subject of Germany before the war.

As usual, it started out frustrating. *There's so much stuff out there and so little you can really use,* she thought, switching to a different search engine. She clicked on sites about World War II, Germany, Nazis. Finally she landed on a site for the Holocaust Project.

She read for a while. Then the screen seemed to blur for a second. Blinking, she realized there were tears in her eyes.

But she kept reading. It was shocking, sickening. But she couldn't tear herself away.

Oh, she'd heard about how the Nazis arrested the Jews during the war. But she'd never seen it so graphically. Here, on web page after web page, she saw the story unfold. First Jews were restricted from public office, then from public life. They were relocated to ghettos, then arrested and herded into boxcars, then transported to concentration camps. There they served in hard labor for the war effort—and many of them were gassed to death.

Six million of them. All because they were Jewish.

How could this happen? she thought.

It wasn't that she'd never heard of discrimination. After all, she was a Latina. In the Anglo parts of town she was followed around in department stores; the managers seemed to assume she was a shoplifter. She'd learned never to give police any reason to shoot her; as Carlos said, "If you're Anglo, you get a chance to explain. If your skin is brown or black, you don't." She knew how hard it had been for her mother to find a job, and Maria herself had been turned down for babysitting assignments by some nervous Anglo parents.

Discrimination was terrible; Maria knew that firsthand. But what she was seeing on her computer screen went beyond anything she'd experienced. Jews in Germany were treated like animals—no, worse than animals.

How could this happen? It wasn't in ancient Mongolia or something, but in Europe just 60 years ago. Weren't people supposed to be civilized in the twentieth century?

She frowned at the screen. It was all Adolf Hitler's doing, wasn't it? He had this insane goal of "purifying" the German race by slaughtering the Jews—and others who didn't fit into his plans. He was a crazy man, in love with his own power and vicious in his use of it.

So how did his Nazi party take power in this supposedly civilized land? How did he become the leader of the German people?

They voted for him.

Maria did a search on Hitler and found that he lost an election in 1930 but tried again. In 1933 the Nazis won the election with 17 million votes—more than twice the amount received by any other party. Hitler became the ruler of Germany, and the rest was history.

Why would people vote for such a lunatic? Maria asked herself. *Didn't they know how awful he was?*

She went to an encyclopedia's website. After a few minutes of hunting, she read: "The German people wanted security, order, and national prestige. To the discontented lower and middle classes, Hitler promised a higher standard of living." Germans were troubled by an economic depression, worried about the spread of Communism, crowded by foreign immigrants taking "their" jobs. So 17 million people voted for a leader who said he'd get rid of the foreigners, fight the Communists, and keep the Jews from controlling the economy.

The majority ruled.

But the majority wasn't right, she thought.

Reading on, Maria learned that some Germans disagreed

with Hitler—but didn't want to get involved. They kept quiet as the atrocities got worse and worse. They let the majority rule. *Kind of like "butterfly" in the chat room—*

For some reason she couldn't stand to read anymore. She logged off, then sat staring at the blank screen.

Sometime later—she wasn't sure how long she'd been staring—Maria was jolted by the ringing of the kitchen phone. Then Sara was pounding on her door, saying, "It's Carlos! Wonder what *he* wants."

On Maria's way down the hall, Sara was beside her all the way, making faces and kissing noises. Maria rolled her eyes.

"Hey, babe, I've been thinking about you." Even over the phone, Carlos was smooth and seductive.

"That's nice." Maria's mind was still back among the web pages.

"Have you been thinking about me, baby?"

"No, I've been thinking about Hitler."

"I *knew* you had another guy."

"I *do* have another guy, Carlos. Your neighbor Jared."

"I know, I know," Carlos said with a laugh. "I was just joking. Hey, you want to come over tonight?"

A few hours earlier she would have said yes. But now she was in a strange mood. "I'm not sure, Carlos."

"Mmm." She could tell Carlos was surprised. He wasn't used to being turned down. "It's that Hitler guy, isn't it?" he asked.

"Um, yes, I guess you could say that."

He was laughing again. "You are such a bad *muchacha*."

"That's what I'm afraid of," Maria replied, with a seriousness that shocked even her. "I'm not sure this is right. You and me."

Carlos stopped laughing. "Right, wrong? What's that?

Every day people go after what they want. Why not us?"

"So if everybody else is okay with that, I should be, too, huh?"

"Well . . ."

"Maybe we should just take a vote. Ask everybody in the neighborhood."

"Hey, babe, how come you're sounding so hostile? Come on over. Just come over, we'll talk about it."

"I'm not sure," Maria said softly. "I'm just not sure. Maybe I'll call you later." Gently she placed the phone in its cradle, her mind full of questions.

AND NOW, BACK TO YOU . . .

"Twenty million people can't be wrong!"

Maybe you've heard a phrase like that on a TV commercial. It's baloney. Of *course* 20 million people can be wrong. It happens all the time.

How about those 17 million people in Germany who voted for Hitler? There were so many of them—and they were so wrong, dead wrong. They brought disaster to Germany, to the Jews, and to the world.

When you were seven, you probably tried the "strength in numbers" argument with your parents.

| **Mother:** | I said no—you're not allowed to eat a candy bar before dinner. |
| **You:** | But all the other kids get to! |

Mother: If all the other kids jumped in a lake, would you?

If it was a hot day, the idea of jumping in a lake sounded pretty good. Still, your mother's point makes sense. You can't let "everybody" tell you what to do. When you follow the crowd, you can end up in some pretty strange places.

Of course, "the crowd" doesn't have to have millions of people in it. It can be just the particular group you most feel a part of.

My friend Griffin is a good example. Smart and talented, he dyed his hair all sorts of colors and wore a mismatched wardrobe that Goodwill might have rejected. Within his circle of artsy friends, he was admired for being *himself.* He didn't care what anyone else thought, and some people loved him for it. Most others in the school just thought he was weird—but he got the "votes" of the kids who mattered to him.

Whether you identify most with the jocks, the choir kids, the computer geeks, the Goths . . . the question is, does a group's majority opinion determine what's true?

Some say yes. There's no such thing as bottom-line truth, they declare. Every society gets to come up with its own. What matters is the "solidarity" of the group, the way it hangs together.

But what if the group hangs together by torturing everyone whose last name begins with "K"? What if the group votes to allow rape? To buy and sell slaves?

What if the group decides next year to reverse its decision? Which decision was right? And on what factors does the group base its decisions in the first place?

If you're looking for truth you can count on, truth that doesn't change, you won't find it by polling a group. Groups are fickle. They pick leaders and crucify them within a week.

Take your graduating class at school, for example. How durable are its values? The state soccer title may seem important to a lot of students now, but in ten years how many will really care who won? Will those voted "Most Likely to Succeed" be on their third divorces? Will the rich clique be paying the computer geeks big bucks to run the world for them? Will the rebels be depressed because they can't find a square inch of skin left to pierce or tattoo?

In other words, can the people around you create truth and meaning and purpose for their lives—and yours—by taking a vote?

It didn't work in Hitler's Germany. Or in all the groups that have given their stamp of approval to things like human sacrifice, cannibalism, slavery, and genocide.

Do you want to put your future to a vote? Or is there a more reliable way to decide what's true?

If there isn't, we're all in big trouble.

Five

Think Pad

WELCOME TO TEENTALK
Screen Name: r2d2
Logon 9:41 P.M.

Hulkster:	Did you see that play? I can't believe they didn't call a penalty.
Tim4U:	Looked like interference to me.
Hulkster:	Everyone in the world saw it—except the refs.
r2d2:	What are you talking about?
Hulkster:	Didn't you watch the big game? Cowboys and Eagles.
nobraner:	football
r2d2:	Oh, no. I'm not into football. But once I did analyze the physics involved in throwing a perfect spiral.
nobraner:	no kidding
r2d2:	It has to do with the trajectory of the ball as it moves across the hand before it's thrown.
Hulkster:	Fascinating. Anyway, that NON-call was a travesty of justice.

r2d2: Well, here's a REAL travesty for you. The school board in my town just voted to force science teachers to stop teaching evolution and teach creationism instead.

Tim4U: So?

r2d2: Don't you see? That's like totally messed up. They can't do that.

nobraner: its their school

r2d2: But it's wrong. They should just let teachers teach science.

Tim4U: But maybe the teachers are teaching more than science.

r2d2: No, that's the point. They want them to start teaching religion. That's not their job. If we want religion, we'll go to a church.

wonderboy: He's got a point there.

r2d2: It's so simple. It's those stupid fundamentalists who are poking their noses into everything. It's about religion. It's about politics. And no one cares about truth anymore.

Tim4U: Maybe they do care about truth.

r2d2: Then why would they keep the teachers from teaching something as basic as evolution? Now they have to say "This is just one theory."

Tim4U: But isn't it?

r2d2: No, that makes it sound like someone just made it up. It's been proven.

nobraner: didn't darwin make it up?

r2d2: He discovered it. He explained it. But it's been proven a million times. It's like a basic building block of natural science.

nobraner:	hey, evolution, creation . . . let the people choose
r2d2:	You guys don't get it. It's fine if people want to believe that some supernatural force created the world in six days, but THAT'S NOT SCIENCE!!! Science teachers shouldn't have to teach that.
Tim4U:	So they should only teach what has been scientifically proven.
r2d2:	Exactly.
Tim4U:	Can they prove that the world wasn't created by God?
r2d2:	That's totally outside the scope of science. It can't be proven one way or the other.
Tim4U:	So science has no right saying there's NOT a God who created the world.
nobraner:	i get it. you're good, bible boy
r2d2:	You're missing the point.
nobraner:	maybe he's getting the point and you aren't
r2d2:	Whose side are you on? You sound like a creationist.
nobraner:	i don't really care. if there is a god, i just wish he'd find some way for me to eat chocolate without gaining weight
Hulkster:	There is a way. It's called exercise.
r2d2:	I can tell you're all more interested in football than in science, but I'm telling you THIS IS WRONG.
Tim4U:	And I don't know much about science, but it seems that after you do all your proving you have to admit that there are some things you can't prove.

r2d2: We can prove that everything in the universe started with a tiny speck that exploded in the Big Bang, creating everything that is.

Hulkster: How can you prove that?

r2d2: It's complicated, but it has to do with physical calculations of the way the universe is expanding. I can give you some book titles if you want to read more about it.

Hulkster: Uh, no thanks.

Tim4U: So you say you can prove that everything started with one event, which you call the Big Bang.

r2d2: Yes.

Tim4U: What caused the Big Bang?

r2d2: Nothing caused it. It just happened.

Tim4U: Can you prove that nothing caused it?

r2d2: No, but we can prove that everything was started by it.

Tim4U: What if I said that God caused the Big Bang?

r2d2: That's religion, not science.

Tim4U: I can't prove God caused it, but you can't prove that ANYTHING caused it. I'm just calling that event Creation.

r2d2: But that's not scicnce!!!

Tim4U: Is it science to think that NOTHING caused the universe? Seems to me that the God idea is at least a possibility.

Hulkster: This is getting way too heavy for me. I'm checking out.

[Hulkster has left the chat room.]

Tim4U: Sorry. Didn't mean to preach at you.

r2d2:	No, that's the thing. You can't help but preach, because you have no intelligent science to back you up. If you really started digging into science, you'd see how impossible most of those Bible stories are.
wonderboy:	Yeah, I think those are a little farfetched.
r2d2:	They're nice fables, but they didn't really happen.
Tim4U:	Can you prove that?
r2d2:	Yes! I mean, miracles—like walking on water or turning water to wine—that stuff just doesn't happen in everyday life.
Tim4U:	That's why they're miracles.
r2d2:	If you want to believe that stuff, fine. Just don't make me listen to it in science class.

REAL LIFE
At the Chemistry Lab with Rob (aka r2d2)
Next Day

After school, Rob headed down to the chem lab as usual. It was his hangout. He usually had a project he could work on there, and some of the other science kids would sometimes drop by. But mainly he looked forward to seeing Mr. Newson.

Not only was Newson the smartest teacher at school, he was the coolest. He had a way of treating students as human beings—a quality all too rare among the teachers at Linhurst High. As a teacher he was inspiring, but in these casual moments after school Mr. Newson was a friend. Rob felt he could talk with him about anything.

Mr. Newson wasn't in the lab yet, so Rob dug out some equipment and began setting up an experiment. He was trying to create amino acids out of basic chemicals found in nature. It was an ambitious project, attempting to answer key questions about how life began on this planet, but Mr. Newson had never discouraged him. Even if the experiment failed, Rob would learn an awful lot. "Failures," the teacher often said, "are the building blocks of science."

About 20 minutes later, Rob was cooking up chemicals when he was startled by footsteps outside the door. Mr. Newson stormed in, threw a folder on a lab table, and then noticed Rob working there. "Sorry to bother you," he said, with a nod toward Rob's foaming beaker. "Is it soup yet?"

"Chicken noodle," Rob smiled. "Want some? It's mmm mmm good."

"No thanks," the teacher answered. "I just walked past the cafeteria and totally lost my appetite."

"I know the feeling," Rob said with a laugh. He turned the flame down on the Bunsen burner and took off his lab goggles. "You . . . uh . . . seemed upset when you came in."

"I was just talking with Miss Runnels about the school board's decision."

"It's crazy," Rob said, shaking his head. "I was online last night in a chat room with some creationist. I can't believe how illogical they are. It just doesn't make any sense."

"Jackie—Miss Runnels—said she might quit."

"I hope she doesn't." Rob knew that Miss Runnels, as a biology teacher, would be greatly affected by the requirement to teach creationism. He wouldn't blame her for leaving, but it would be a great loss. Not just because she was one of the nicest teachers at Linhurst, but because she'd been going out with Mr. Newson.

"I can't believe they're actually going through with it," Mr. Newson was saying as he paced behind the long lab table at the front of the room. "When I spoke at the school board meeting, they asked me to defend evolution. Can you believe that? *Defend* evolution."

"Yeah, you told me."

"I thought I had them convinced. What a bunch of—well, never mind."

Rob had never seen his teacher so agitated. He wished he could help somehow.

He tried reason. "Look at it logically. That's what you've always taught me."

"There *is* no logic to it."

"There's always logic. You said that the first week of class. Now, what do we observe? The school board doing something that makes no sense."

"That makes no sense *to us*," the teacher corrected.

"Of course. So, anyway—"

"Otherwise you're implying that there's an absolute standard that they're violating."

"Well, aren't they?"

The teacher looked upward, as he did when considering tough questions. "We don't know that yet."

"All right. So the school board does something that makes no sense *to us*. What could be the cause of this phenomenon? Some sort of alien invasion?"

Mr. Newson cracked a smile. "That's a theory," he said. "How do we prove it?"

"We can't, so let's try another theory."

"Why can't we?"

Rob squinted. "Because, well—"

"Because it's outside the system."

"I guess so. Which means . . . "

Mr. Newson gazed out the window to the courtyard, where a few cheerleaders were practicing their moves. "Which means we don't know. We can't prove, we can't disprove."

"Okay. Putting aside the question of aliens, let's use the scientific method. Now, we also observe that the most outspoken board members are religious, which would indicate their motives are clearly in the direction of religious indoctrination, which goes against the First Amend—"

"Do you really think science can do that?"

"Do what?"

Mr. Newson absently ran a finger along the lab table. "Tell us what to do. I know science can tell us what *is*, and maybe how it got there, but can it really tell us what to do? For example, can it tell me . . . I mean, tell *anyone* whether a person is truly in love?"

Rob gulped. Something told him this wasn't about anybody hypothetical. It was about Miss Runnels.

"How do we decide what to do in relationships? If someone you care for quits and moves away, should you go, too? What is love? Are there any chemicals in it?"

Rob had heard about nervous breakdowns, and wondered if that was happening before his eyes.

"The scientific method only goes so far. Causes remain a mystery. If we say that A always causes B, we can use an experiment to disprove that idea if we have A without B or B without A, but if we have A and B, what does that mean? Who's to say which caused which? And who's to say that the hundredth or thousandth time it won't be different? Are you following me?"

"Yes," Rob lied. He realized he wasn't going to get much done on his experiment, so he turned off the burner and began packing it up.

"And who's to say," Mr. Newson went on, "that those chemicals in that beaker aren't arguing about which of them caused the other one, or whether some scientist up there stirred them all together? But that would be outside the system."

The teacher fastened his gaze on Rob. "Don't get me wrong. I believe in science with all my heart. Everything I've taught you is absolutely true—*inside the system*. But *outside* the system . . . " His voice just trailed off.

The silence hung heavy in the air, along with the sharp smell of the chemicals Rob had been heating.

Finally the teacher cleared his throat. "Look, Rob, I hope I didn't ruin your afternoon. I'm sure the whole school board thing will work itself out eventually. I've got to get these papers down to the office."

"I just need to wash up and then I'm going," Rob said. "I'll see you tomorrow." As Mr. Newson hurried out of the lab with a folder under his arm, Rob poured the contents of the beaker down the drain.

AND NOW, BACK TO YOU . . .

How do you find ultimate truth?

Through your feelings? Well, we saw in Chapter 3 that feelings can't give us reliable answers to math tests or questions about how to act on our appetites.

Through public opinion? Chapter 4 brought up the little problem of how groups sometimes vote to do some pretty terrible things.

That leaves reason, right? It seems only logical that we should be able to find our way to truth simply by using our brains to interpret what we can see, touch, smell, taste, and hear.

But it's not that simple.

If we could think and experiment our way to all truth, the smartest people on earth would have all the answers. The leading philosophers and scientists would have it all figured out.

But that's not the case. Many of the world's best thinkers are just as confused as its worst thinkers. All their answers lead to more questions.

Take Mr. Newson. He's a fictional character, of course, but he represents a lot of thinkers. If they're honest with themselves, they eventually realize how much they *don't* know. They look for proof, but all they have is guesswork. Theories build on other theories that supposedly explain the way things are, but all it takes is one Einstein to blow the whole thing into chaos—relatively speaking.

Does that mean you shouldn't use your mind? Of course not. Reason is one of the best tools we have to understand ultimate truth. We should be logical, even scientific, in the way we view the world. Thinking is a good thing.

The problem comes when people assume they can figure out *everything*. If you can't measure it scientifically, they say, it doesn't exist. If it's outside their mental grid, it's not worth talking about.

As Dr. Doug Geivett, Biola University philosophy professor, explains, the trouble isn't with reason—but with the way some people define and apply it. Until fairly recently, he says, scientists generally accepted certain limits for scientific explanation—and left it to other specialists like philosophers and theologians to deal with the rest.

"But now," he says, "there are scientists who think all that can be known is what science can tell us, and they have tried to push the boundaries of scientific explanation further." One physicist, for instance, claims that science can show the universe has a beginning—but no cause.

Dr. Geivett concludes, "We need to ask the question: Can science lead us to God? I would argue that science can lead us to make a reasonable inference to the existence of God as the best explanation for many things that science cannot otherwise explain—including the origin of the universe."

Let's take that little matter of how the universe came to be. Scientists have done great work in following the astronomical evidence and tracing everything back to a theoretical "Big Bang." They've deduced logically that the universe began in that one cataclysmic moment. Assuming that's what happened, what caused the Big Bang?

That's where you come to a fork in the road. If you're willing to allow for the possibility that the supernatural exists you can say that a Creator caused it. But if you assume that the natural world is all that is or ever will be, then you have to say, "There must be a physical answer, but we haven't found it yet."

Either way, you're using reason—and using it to reach conclusions based on more than just the physical evidence you have.

That's a problem with the theory of evolution, too. When you look at the evidence, it's amazing how little of Darwin's plan has actually been proven. We can see microevolution—

natural selection on a small scale, within various species. But the idea that reptiles became birds or that apes and humans had a common ancestor—that's a huge theory with little or no evidence. Why do you think the "missing links" are missing?

Recently one supposed "missing link" skeleton turned out to be a fake. A leading scientist commented, "Apparently this wasn't it, but we're sure we'll find it."

Now *there's* an assumption.

Some believe in a God outside the "natural" system; others believe only in the system. The latter put their trust in Darwin or in other theories that aren't proven *yet*. But they all assume something—thereby reinforcing the idea that physical evidence can only take you so far.

Science is great at answering the *what* and *how* questions. But it can't answer the really big questions of *who* and *why*. To answer those, we have the option of looking beyond the physical evidence we've been able to gather—unless we insist on making the unprovable assumption that the "natural" system is all there is. We can reasonably go "outside the system" for final answers about what's true.

But how?

Early in 2000, several leading websites were temporarily hampered by computer hackers. The FBI launched a thorough investigation. First they employed all their usual evidence-finding techniques. Was there a computer trail? Did the hackers leave electronic "footprints" in the sites they ravaged? No. These culprits knew what they were doing. The FBI had truckloads of data, but few conclusions. They could put together a profile, but they couldn't name names.

At that point, they waited—for someone to talk. In a case like this, an FBI agent explained, hackers do it for the bragging rights. It's only a matter of time before one of the perpetrators starts boasting to a friend in a lunchroom or chat room, "Guess who I hacked." With that revelation, the FBI would finally be able to determine who was responsible.

We're like the investigators. We've examined the evidence and reached our limit. We may have bits and pieces of a profile, but no name.

We need someone to talk. We need revelation.

Some would say that's where God comes in. They believe He *has* talked, extensively, about who we are, where we've come from, and where we're going. And about truth—absolute truth.

Six

The Webmaster

WELCOME TO TEENTALK
Screen Name: nobraner
Logon 7:22 P.M.

nobraner:	So, how are carlos and that other guy?
butterfly:	I feel so guilty sometimes. I try to stop seeing Carlos, but I can't.
Hulkster:	Is this just girl talk, or can I jump in?
nobraner:	at your own risk
butterfly:	I'm sure you've got more serious things than my soap opera
Hulkster:	Not really. My life is football.
nobraner:	ugh
Hulkster:	And Jonica.
butterfly:	Girlfriend?
Hulkster:	Well, she was. She broke up with me.
butterfly:	Wasn't your type of girl, huh?
Hulkster:	I guess I wasn't her type of guy.
	[mullmore has entered the chat room.]
butterfly:	What do you mean?
Hulkster:	I kept making decisions that made football

	the most important thing in my life, and she didn't like that.
butterfly:	And you're trying to get her back
Hulkster:	If I can. I miss her a lot.
mullmore:	Sometimes we don't know what we have until we stop having it.
nobraner:	thank you, mullmore. who are you?
butterfly:	I like that saying.
nobraner:	ever heard of joni mitchell?
mullmore:	I am only what I say, as are you.
Hulkster:	I guess we all are, when we're online. [Tim4U has entered the chat room.]
Tim4U:	Hey, guys, what's up?
nobraner:	the mysterious mullmore is quoting folk songs
Tim4U:	Who's mullmore?
butterfly:	Get this. He is what he says.
Tim4U:	What does he say?
mullmore:	Guilt is a waste of time unless it leads to redemption.
nobraner:	see what I mean?
Tim4U:	He's got a point there.
nobraner:	not you too! i heard that line on one of my mom's billy joel records
butterfly:	Relax, nb. He's not doing any harm.
nobraner:	how do we know it's a he?
Hulkster:	We don't.
Tim4U:	Mullmore, are you male or female?
butterfly:	he sounds like a guy.
Hulkster:	Why do you say that?
nobraner:	no girl would be that pretentious

butterfly:	No, he just talks like a wise man. Like Buddha, or even Jesus.
Tim4U:	Come on, mullmore, quit lurking and reveal your identity.
mullmore:	Gender is a distraction. Perceive the heart.
butterfly:	That is so great! He talks, like, in posters.
nobraner:	i'd hate to see the walls of your room
Hulkster:	I think he's weird—he or she.
Tim4U:	Let's just pretend he's not there and have a normal conversation.
Hulkster:	Good idea.
Tim4U:	So what's this about guilt? Who's feeling guilty about what?
Hulkster:	I don't want to talk about it.
nobraner:	his heart is still hurting from a breakup
Tim4U:	Sorry to hear that.
nobraner:	and butterfly knows she should break up but can't
butterfly:	I don't want to talk about it.
Tim4U:	That's what I love about chat rooms. People just talk about everything.
Hulkster:	I have a dentist appointment tomorrow.
nobraner:	I'd rather talk about mullmore
mullmore:	Remember, friends, every person has a wound. Goodnight.
	[mullmore has left the chat room.]
nobraner:	at last!
butterfly:	I liked him . . . or her.
nobraner:	are you writing this stuff down?
butterfly:	Yes, I'm copying and saving those sayings to my hard drive.

nobraner: and putting them to music, no doubt

butterfly: I think they're wise. We can all use some help in thinking a bit deeper about life.

nobraner: but that's not deep. that's reader's digest.

Hulkster: What's wrong with Reader's Digest?

nobraner: i just hate it when anyone tries to make life simpler than it is

Hulkster: I like the jokes in that magazine.

nobraner: buddha, jesus, mullmore—whoever it is, i don't care. i just don't want anybody telling me how to live my life.

Tim4U: Did you throw Jesus in there with mullmore?

nobraner: you have a problem with that?

Tim4U: I do.

nobraner: i thought you might

Tim4U: Have you ever really read what Jesus said? It would be one thing if your life was perfect and fulfilling already, but I seem to remember you being pretty depressed not long ago. I think Jesus might have some ideas that could help you. I know I'd be pretty messed up if it weren't for Jesus.

nobraner: well, thanks again, bible boy, for that stirring sermon. you and mullmore make quite a pair.

Tim4U: Sorry. Sometimes I don't know when to stop.

nobraner: funny, i started tonight in a good mood, but now i'm feeling down again. Too many philosophers.

[nobraner has left the chat room.]

REAL LIFE
The Home of Julie (aka nobraner)
That Night

Julie lay awake half the night, listening to her heart. She just could not get to sleep. She tried counting sheep; she tried counting songs with the word "baby" in them; she tried counting prime numbers up to a thousand. Nothing worked.

Words kept crowding out the numbers. Bits of "mullmore's" sayings crept into her head and got jumbled. *Guilt is a distraction unless it leads to being wounded. Or something like that.*

Who was that person? she thought. *Some guru wannabe who can't afford a saffron robe?* It was easy to *sound* wise, but did this "mullmore" know the magic words that could chase away the overwhelming sense of *nothing* in her soul?

And then there was Bible boy, Tim something, always pushing his church thing a bit too hard. Not a bad guy, as far as she could tell, but he didn't know when to back off. What was that he'd said? "I seem to remember you being depressed. I think Jesus could help you."

Right, she thought. *Like I'm going to sign up for the born-again club and become one of the Jesus clones.* They were hypocrites with big hair who clucked at you whenever you said a bad word. Did Tim think they could rescue her?

I don't think so, she thought, rolling over in bed and trying for the millionth time to get to sleep.

What else had Tim said? "I'd be pretty messed up if it weren't for Jesus." *Uh-huh.* Tim didn't know what messed-up was. He could probably *use* some messing up; he seemed to have everything in place.

She thought of her brother, James. Now *he* was messed up, big time. In a perpetual haze, he was wasting his college years on booze, bongs, and babes. She tried to imagine James as a Jesus freak and laughed out loud.

And where was she? Somewhere between totally messed up and totally perfect—and sinking fast. She needed a "mullmore" who actually made sense, someone with substance behind the fancy words. Someone who could give her something to live for. Maybe even help her get to sleep.

"Jesus could help you." The letters kept scrolling across the screen of her closed eyes. "Jesus could help you."

All right, Jesus, she thought. *You want to help me? Help me get to sleep!*

Sometime later, light poked into her consciousness. Her room was way too bright. Julie propped open an eye and tried to figure out what was wrong. The sounds were different—different birds, different traffic. She rolled over to check her alarm clock. Ten-thirteen. *Oh.* She rolled back to her pillow.

TEN-THIRTEEN? She sat up fast. *I'm late. How did that happen?* She must have slept through her alarm, or forgotten to set it. *Mom probably knocked on the door when she left for work, but I never heard it.*

Running down the hall to the shower, Julie tried to calculate how quickly she could get to school. Halfway through third period? No way. All right, fourth period. She could still make her lit class, but she'd missed her geometry test. *Maybe that's not such a bad thing.* She'd have to sign in late, and without a note she might get detention, unless she could sweet-talk Miss Corcoran. But the woman had a will of titanium.

The school was within walking distance, and it was a nice day, so Julie set off on foot. Not that she had much choice—what with a license but no car, and her folks already at their jobs in the city.

But it was a nice walk. Halfway to school, she suddenly realized, *I feel great!* The sleep had done her good. What had she done to fall asleep? Counting things? No, that never worked. Taking her mom's pills? No; she'd thought about it, but didn't.

Oh, no, it couldn't be. She smiled as she remembered thinking about Jesus. She'd actually asked—no, she'd *challenged* Him to help her sleep. *What a coincidence. I try praying for the first time in a decade, and boom, I'm out like a light. Go figure.*

Maybe it wasn't a coincidence. The thought jabbed at her as she approached the school. She would fend it off, but it would enter another corner of her consciousness. *Maybe it worked.*

Should she try it out again? How? If Jesus had some kind of power, how would He show it in her life? Would He appear suddenly next to her in the cafeteria? Would He convince Miss Corcoran to let her in late? Would He make her zits disappear?

That was ridiculous. Whoever Jesus was, He wasn't a magic charm that solved all your problems.

Try again, said a thought that came to her. She stepped through the big front doors of the school building. *Okay. You want to help me, Jesus? Go ahead. Do something.*

The attendance office was empty when she arrived. For a moment she thought she might be excused, but then Miss Corcoran lumbered in from a side office. "Got a note?" she barked.

"No," Julie replied. "I slept through my alarm." She

searched for some crevice of sympathy in the woman's face.

"Hrrrumph!" went Miss Corcoran, not unlike a seal. "That's a detention. Room 1013, today or tomorrow, 3:00 P.M."

"Tomorrow," Julie said, and grabbed the pink pass the attendance officer was thrusting toward her.

She slipped into fourth-period literature a few minutes late, waving the pass at the teacher, who nodded. At the end of the class the teacher announced another project—picking any twentieth-century author and discussing his or her view of the meaning of life, in five pages. Students could team up if they wanted.

In the cafeteria, Julie had just gotten up the nerve to dig into her school-issued beef stroganoff when Sheri sat down beside her. "Ya wanna be a team?" Sheri asked cheerily. Her high-pitched voice didn't seem to grate as much as usual.

"Oh, hi, Sheri. How are you? I'm fine. What was that you wanted?"

Sheri giggled and shrugged. "Sorry. I do kind of jump right in there, don't I? But I wanted to know if you'd like to team up again for lit class. We did pretty well, I thought, with that *Waiting for God* thing."

"*Godot,*" Julie corrected, emphasizing the long French "o." She looked at Sheri, pondering. Yes, Sheri gave the impression that she was auditioning to be the next bimbo on some *Baywatch* spinoff. But she wasn't as dumb as she seemed. On their last project, Julie had sunk into a brain-sapping despair and Sheri had ended up doing most of the work. *I owe her,* Julie thought.

"Sure," she said. "That sounds good."

"Ya wanna come over this afternoon and start working on it?" Sheri asked.

"Let me check my social calendar." Julie gazed into the air for exactly one second and then said, "Fine. I have no life."

"Good. I'll meet you at your locker after school," Sheri bubbled, then waved a pale green stalk in front of Julie. "Want some celery?"

"I don't know," Julie answered, looking down at her tray of stroganoff. "Fat and starch or veggies? Tough call, but I'll go with the fat and starch. Wait . . . what's that on your wrist?"

Sheri pulled the celery back and rotated the leather band on her wrist. "Just a bracelet."

"But leather? That's not your usual style."

"It's just something my mom gave me," Sheri said apologetically.

Julie took Sheri's arm to examine the band more closely. "I like it. But what does it say? *W.W.J.D.* I've seen that before. What does it mean?"

"'What Would Jesus Do?'"

Julie gasped. It was as if Jesus had sat down next to her in the cafeteria. "So . . . are you a Christian?"

"Well," Sheri drawled, rolling her eyes a bit, "yes, I am. But I'm not . . . like . . . you know."

"It's okay," Julie reassured her. "It's just fine."

After school they met at Julie's locker and walked to Sheri's house. Julie hesitated to ask about Jesus, but her curiosity was too much. They'd just started talking about their meaning-of-life project when Julie finally blurted out, "So, does Jesus give you meaning for *your* life?"

"Huh?" Sheri asked, wide-eyed.

"Does He make any difference? Does He make life more livable? Or is this just some sort of club you join where you wear cool bracelets?"

"Well, He's, like, my Savior. I asked Him into my heart and He gave me eternal life."

"But what does that *mean,* Sheri? How does that make your life better?"

Sheri looked like a contestant on *Jeopardy* who kept pressing the button but nothing happened. "I really haven't thought about that very much."

"Then think about it!" Julie nearly shouted. "I need to know!"

"I'm sorry, Julie. I wish I could say the right things for you, but—wait." Sheri's eyes fixed on her bookshelf. There, under some novels and a magazine, was a red leather-bound Bible. Sheri sprang up to get it. "Here. This will tell you everything you want to know."

Julie handled the book as if it were radioactive, carefully opening it and turning a few flimsy pages.

"Oh," Sheri said, "but don't start at the front. That's the Old Testament. You want the Gospels. Here." The Bible had a scarlet ribbon attached to its binding, which Sheri placed at the beginning of Matthew. "This will tell you about Jesus."

AND NOW, BACK TO YOU . . .

It happens every two or three years in the high school drama department.

Auditions are held for the spring musical. Some kid who's always been in the chorus—third soprano from the left in the back row—tries out for a leading role. Something has happened to her since the last play, and now she takes the stage with confidence. She sings a song that has the director, musical director, and assistants openly weeping. People stop in the hallway and crowd around the stage door to catch a glimpse of this prodigy. Suddenly this girl that no one noticed before is commanding everyone's attention. She is something special.

Sometimes it happens like that when people start to pay attention to Jesus. They're used to thinking of Him as the "third religious leader from the left"—next to Buddha, Moses, and Mohammed. But then something happens.

Maybe they see a show like *Godspell*, which portrays Jesus as someone who liked to have fun but who also defied authority, and they want to learn more. Or maybe someone hands them a Bible and they start to read it.

Whatever the reason, they begin to look into who Jesus really is. And the real Jesus knocks their socks off.

Remember the computer hacker investigation in the last chapter? FBI agents gathered evidence, assembled a profile— and ran into a brick wall. They had to wait for the culprits to identify themselves. Somebody had to talk. In our quest for ultimate truth, we have to do the same thing—using our feelings, the opinions of others, and our own thinking to assemble a profile. But those things can take us only so far. To solve this case, we have to wait for someone to talk—someone who really knows the answers.

Well, Jesus is talking. Let's listen to His voice—and see if He matches the profile of truth.

What do we need to know about Jesus? Here are six important facts.

First, *He was Jewish*. That's ironic when you think of all the bad things so-called Christians have done to Jews over the years, but Christianity was originally Jewish. What does that mean? Well, the Jews believed there was only one God, while other nations had entire menus of gods to follow. The Jews also believed that this God loved them and wanted a relationship with them. In other nations, gods were feared and worshiped and sacrificed to. The Jews did these things, too, but the idea of a God who loved His people was unusual.

The Jews also believed that God had given them specific guidelines about how to live. They didn't always follow these rules, but they knew God wanted them to. They recognized that the world was messed up because people didn't live God's way, and they looked forward to a special person—the Messiah—who would come and make everything right between God and His people.

Jesus grew up in a Jewish town called Nazareth. He worked as a carpenter, but also became known as a teacher, a rabbi. One day in His hometown synagogue He read aloud the Scripture—a section about the Messiah. Instead of preaching about it, He said, "Today this scripture is fulfilled in your hearing" (Luke 4:21). In other words, "The Messiah is standing right in front of you."

This is the second thing we need to know about Jesus: *He spoke His mind.* When He saw the religious leaders being self-righteous and hypocritical, He said so. But He also challenged His closest friends.

Some people seem to think Jesus was easygoing, but He actually set standards that were even harder than the Jewish rules. The rule was: Don't kill. Jesus said: Don't even hate. The rule was: Don't have sex with someone you're not married to. Jesus said: Don't even think about it. The rule was: Love your neighbor. Jesus said: Love your enemy, too.

Jesus was careful not to come right out and say, "I am the

Messiah"—which would have gotten Him killed way before His time. But He dropped plenty of hints. When one follower asked for a way to heaven, Jesus replied, "I am the way and the truth and the life. No one comes to the Father except through me" (John 14:6).

That's pretty strong stuff, unless you can back it up. Jesus was saying He's the doorman of heaven, and you can't get in unless He stamps your hand. No one else made the claims Jesus did—and no one else could back them up as He did.

That brings us to the third point: *Jesus displayed awesome power.* He stopped storms. He turned water to wine. He fed a crowd with a bag lunch. And He healed people—lots of people. He even brought some back from the dead. There was supernatural power flowing through this Man. Something big was going on here.

You might be wondering, "Why should I believe all this about Jesus? *Who says* He displayed awesome power? The Bible. And what if the Bible is just a bunch of made-up stories?"

Good point. We'll deal more with that question in the next chapter. For now, let's just consider who would have made up these stories: the disciples of Jesus. If they'd devoted their lives to following a Teacher who said, "I am the truth," would they make up lies about Him? Probably not. But even if they did, would they stick with these lies even when threatened with death? Tradition has it that 10 of the original 12 disciples were killed because of their faith. Would they have died for something they knew was a lie?

Fourth, *Jesus' message applied to everybody.* The truth He brought wasn't just meant for His own country or ethnic group or a little set of religious experts. In fact, He nailed the religious leaders of His day for making it hard for "outsiders" to know

God. He told those experts, "I tell you the truth, the tax collectors and the prostitutes are entering the kingdom of God ahead of you" (Matthew 21:31). If we're looking for truth, it has to be truth that crosses centuries and boundaries—all the way to us.

Fifth, *Jesus taught with amazing wisdom*. He told stories based on everyday life, but they were really about much more. His words were simple, but packed a punch.

"Do to others as you would have them do to you" (Luke 6:31).

"No one can serve two masters" (Matthew 6:24).

"What good will it be for a man if he gains the whole world, yet forfeits his soul?" (Matthew 16:26)

"For he who is least among you all—he is the greatest" (Luke 9:48).

"Give to Caesar what is Caesar's, and to God what is God's" (Matthew 22:21).

That's just a smattering of the sound bites in the Gospels. Read more for yourself, and you may agree that Jesus' teachings have the ring of truth. They touch something deep in our souls.

Sixth—and lastly—*Jesus* was *His message*. He taught about love—and showed love to everyone around Him. He taught about the kingdom of God—and stayed true to it even when the kingdom of this world crucified Him. He taught about the power of God—and, according to the Bible, that power raised Him from the dead.

Many people of different religions revere Jesus as a great teacher, but it seems He was far more than that.

If the Bible is correct, He didn't just teach the truth. He *was*—and *is*—the truth.

If that's the case, any hunt for ultimate truth must lead in His direction.

Seven

You've Got Mail

WELCOME TO TEENTALK
Screen Name: nobraner
Logon 8:30 P.M.

r2d2:	So now ALL the teachers are talking about quitting.
wonderboy:	That's bad.
Tim4U:	Hey, everyone. What's up?
nobraner:	i'm glad you're here, tim
Tim4U:	You are? I thought I was preaching at you too much.
nobraner:	you were, but that doesn't matter now
Tim4U:	What's up?
nobraner:	i got a bible
Tim4U:	You did?
r2d2:	A Bible?
nobraner:	yes, a bible. What's so strange about that?
Tim4U:	Nothing. I just thought you were against all that.
nobraner:	i did, too
r2d2:	So now you're born again or something?

nobraner: no!!!! i'm just looking into the bible. i want to find out about jesus

r2d2:   So nobraner is a Jesus freak.

Tim4U: There's nothing wrong with that.

nobraner: i'm not!!! stop saying that!!!

r2d2:   I just thought you had a little more intelligence than that.

Tim4U: What's that supposed to mean?

r2d2:   Look, I've got a bunch of knee-jerk fundies in my town trying to throw away 300 years of science. I don't mean anything personal against you, Tim4U, but in my experience Jesus freaks aren't the swiftest people around.

nobraner: i'm not saying anything about science. i'm just trying to learn about a historical figure i know nothing about. is that ok with you?

r2d2:   Fine. Just be careful.

nobraner: so, tim, i started reading matthew and i don't get it. first it's a bunch of names, then it's like christmas, but they're killing babies, and then john starts baptizing people and yelling at them

[butterfly has entered the chat room]

nobraner: he calls them snakes

wonderboy: That reminds me. What's the most dangerous part of a snake charmer's car? Viper blades!

r2d2:   [deafening silence]

wonderboy: Sorry.

butterfly: Why are you talking about snakes?

r2d2:   Nobraner says it's in the Bible.

butterfly:	You're reading the Bible?
r2d2:	Shocking, ain't it?
butterfly:	No, I think that's a good thing.
wonderboy:	As long as it's not contagious.
Tim4U:	What are you looking for, nobraner?
nobraner:	jesus
Tim4U:	Well, you're close. Just keep going in Matthew. Soon John baptizes Jesus.
r2d2:	I can't believe our chat room has turned into Sunday school.
Tim4U:	Pretty soon you'll get Jesus' Sermon on the Mount. After that you might want to flip over to the Gospel of John.
nobraner:	where's that?
Tim4U:	Matthew, Mark, Luke, John.
wonderboy:	The original Beatles.
r2d2:	I can't believe you're actually reading that stuff.
nobraner:	what's wrong with reading it? how else can i learn?
r2d2:	But don't you know that's all a bunch of religious hogwash? It's just fables people made up. It's all been disproven.
Tim4U:	How?
butterfly:	But it gives people peace of mind.
Tim4U:	How has it been disproven?
r2d2:	Come on!!! Walking on water??? Get real.
Tim4U:	It's a miracle. Doesn't mean it couldn't happen. Don't you believe in miracles?
r2d2:	No.
nobraner:	will you guys quit arguing? it makes me want to forget the whole thing

r2d2:   Good.

                [nobraner has left the chat room.]

wonderboy: See what you did?

r2d2:   Wasn't me.

REAL LIFE
Home of Julie (aka nobraner)
That Night

Julie logged off the computer and picked up the red Bible Sheri had given her. She sat at her desk and opened the book to the place marked by the scarlet ribbon. Matthew chapter 3. There was good old John the Baptist, and there were the vipers, and a few verses later . . . Jesus appears. Not a baby in a manger, but a real, live, grown-up Jesus, talking with John about getting baptized.

She didn't understand all this, but read further. The Spirit of God was flying down like a dove and a voice was thundering from heaven. *That's a bit much*, Julie thought. It reminded her of a TV special with magician David Copperfield—birds flying around, strange noises. Was that all Jesus was, a magician?

Suddenly uncomfortable at her desk, Julie went downstairs for a glass of water. As she carried the drink back up to her room, she imagined the magician Jesus turning it into wine. Could He really do that? Would He? If He really helped her get to sleep, and brought Sheri to her when she needed a Bible, what else could He do? Could He turn her *nothing* life into sparkling cider?

Or was it all coincidence and fable?

She set the water on her nightstand, grabbed the Bible, and reclined on her bed, reading further. She wanted to get to Jesus' teaching. What did this wise man actually say? Chapter 4 put Jesus in the desert, being tempted by the devil. This sounded even more like a fable; Julie nearly put the Bible down, but then noticed a familiar phrase.

"Man does not live on bread alone." *So that's where it came from.*

The devil was challenging Jesus, who had been going without food, to turn stones into bread. *Okay, Mr. Copperfield, let's see some magic.* But Jesus refused to put on a show. He just said, "Man does not live on bread alone, but on every word that comes from the mouth of God" (Matthew 4:4). Finally a wise saying from this guru, but what did it mean?

Julie frowned, thinking. *Bread is food. Without food, we die.* But Jesus was saying something else is just as important to our lives, maybe even more important—the words that God says.

She felt a sudden pang of emptiness, the feeling she'd been fighting for several months. *Is this the cure?* she wondered. *Do the words of God replace the nothing in me?*

It was a crazy notion, and she quickly shrugged it off. She was just exploring right now, like a scientist trying to discover the nature of a thing. *Don't jump to conclusions.*

In chapter 5 of Matthew, she found that Sermon on the Mount "Tim4U" had talked about. Her forehead crinkled as she began to unpack the cryptic sayings. "Blessed are the poor in spirit, for theirs is the kingdom of heaven" (Matthew 5:3).

Poor in spirit? What's that? Maybe really "holy" people were "rich in spirit"—so "poor in spirit" must be the opposite, unsure about spiritual stuff, feeling far from God. *That's me. I'm blessed, huh?*

She didn't feel blessed, just sleepy. Jesus went on, blessing those who mourn, the meek, those who hunger and thirst for righteousness. Her eyes slowly closed. *I know I'm hungering and thirsting for something.* With Jesus' words bouncing around her brain, she drifted off to sleep.

She dreamt about food, lots and lots of wonderful food.

The rays of morning tickled her eyelids half a minute before her clock radio came on. It took her a moment to realize she'd slept in her clothes.

She noticed the Bible, still open beside her, and slowly recalled reading it the night before. Either it was very boring or very calming; she'd slept like a stone. *Hope I didn't drool on the pages.* Placing the Bible on the floor by her bed, she got up.

The school day was uneventful. She survived detention, sitting in a classroom with what seemed to be a motorcycle gang. On the way home she saw her mom's car in the driveway. *Strange*, she thought. *Mom is never home this early.*

Julie found her sitting in the kitchen, smoking. "What are you doing home?" Julie asked.

Her mother eyed her with concern. Julie instinctively felt guilty, though she had no idea what for. "We had a business meeting out in Helmwood," her mother explained, pausing to take a drag on the cigarette. "It was silly to go all the way back to the office."

"Oh," said Julie, trying to seem nonchalant—which she would be, except for the strange look she was getting.

"I stopped at the mall to do some shopping," her mother added. "I got you a sweater. It's on your bed."

Bed. Bedroom. She went in my room. Is there anything wrong with my room? Julie scoured her mind to figure out what the problem was. "That's nice," she replied. "Thank you. I'll go look at it."

"Julie, dear." Her mother's words stopped her before she could escape the kitchen. "Is there anything wrong?"

"Wrong? No."

"I know I haven't spent a lot of time at home lately, but I try to make up for it."

"That's okay, Mom. I haven't had a lot of free time myself."

"You know, dear, that if there's anything you need to talk about, I'm there for you. You have my new pager number, don't you?"

"Yes, Mom. It's in my purse."

"You can be totally honest with me. Anything at all. I won't judge you." The cigarette smoke was swirling above her mother's head, giving the impression that she was in some misty swamp.

"Thanks, Mom. I know."

"Julie . . . honey . . . are you in a . . . cult?"

Julie choked back a laugh. "A cult? Of course not!"

"I saw it, you know."

"You saw what?"

"You don't have to pretend with me, darling. Maybe it's some secret thing you're not allowed to talk about. But I hope we can get to the underlying problems. I don't want to lose you."

What did she find? Julie thought. *A bottle of sleeping pills? A video of a friend's weird class project? What?*

"Calm down, Mom, you're not losing me," Julie said, taking a seat at the table. "What did you see in my room?"

"It was there by your bed. A *Bible*."

The more Julie tried to explain, the more her mother misunderstood. Why would her darling daughter need to read such a book? Wasn't her life satisfying enough? *Well, no,* Julie answered, and Mom took it as a personal attack on their way of life.

By the time Julie left the kitchen, Mom seemed convinced that her daughter *was* in a cult—one that memorized the Bible, swore its members to secrecy, and that probably planned to hitchhike to a commune in Roswell, New Mexico and await the arrival of the mother ship.

Julie slammed the door of her room and took ten deep breaths. She saw the sweater on her bed, a tan thing with embroidered flowers—not her color, not her style, probably not even her size. *Mom never listens.* She threw it in the corner. Then her eyes fell upon the Bible. Wouldn't that be a cool act of revenge, letting her mother drive her back into it?

The red ribbon was lodged in Matthew 5, and she skimmed a few pages. Nothing registered; her mind was still racing from the argument. She was already in chapter 10 when her eyes fixed on verse 35: "For I have come to turn 'a man against his father, a daughter against her mother.'"

Julie read it again to make sure she got it right. *Hmm.* Hardly what you'd expect from an "all you need is love" Jesus, but it was exactly what had just happened in the kitchen. The mere presence of a Bible, containing the words of Jesus, had made Julie's mom go ballistic. What *was* it about this book?

She read on. In verse 39 she found Jesus saying, "Whoever finds his life will lose it, and whoever loses his life for my sake will find it." Julie thought of her mother, so intent on "finding herself." The woman had a great career, but there was something very sad about her. Maybe she had found her life, but she had lost it, too.

It was weird, Julie thought, that this 2,000-year-old philosopher would so perfectly describe life in her suburban split-level.

She read ravenously onward, wondering why Jesus scared her mother so much, and searching for any truths that might fill the hole in her own soul.

AND NOW, BACK TO YOU . . .

A lot of people get turned on to Jesus, but then get turned off by the Bible.

Like Julie, they like the way Jesus challenged authority, the way He spoke simple truths in deep ways, even the way He told stories. But when they face the rest of the Bible, they become more like Julie's mom—afraid that it's a weird collection of rules and rituals that will just lead a person off the deep end.

If people are interested enough to crack open a Bible, they soon get a whiff of its strange stories—donkeys talking, big fish swallowing people, a man walking on water—and they tune out. How can those fanciful tales be true?

Some Christians try to answer that question by quoting Scripture to prove Scripture. "Here, look at 2 Timothy 3:16! It says that all Scripture is inspired by God. Doesn't that settle the issue?" Well, not really. It only shows there's a book that claims it's special—but any book could make that claim.

What would happen if someone came to you with the *Book of Alphonse*, which claimed that a school janitor named Alphonse was really the High Huzzah of the Universe and everything he said was a pearl of divine wisdom? You'd be a bit skeptical, and rightfully so. "But look," the Alphonsian might reply, "it says in Alphonse 3:16 that every word in this book is true. Doesn't that prove that you should accept the religion of Alphonse?" Uh, no.

Any book making such a claim has to back it up. Even the Bible.

So what makes the Bible believable? Dr. J.P. Moreland, professor of theology at Talbot Seminary, gives three reasons to trust the Bible. "First," he says, "there's *historical evidence* that the miracles in the Bible really happened."

But how do we know that *anything* in the Bible really happened? For one thing, archaeological evidence keeps confirming details of biblical stories. For example:

- Scholars used to doubt that Old Testament character David really existed, but recent digs have found his name inscribed on ancient stones.
- Experts used to scoff at the idea that Moses wrote the "books of Moses"—the first five books of the Bible— because supposedly no one knew how to write back then. Wrong again. Examples of early writing have been found in Egypt and elsewhere, and if Moses was educated in Pharaoh's court, he surely would have had that skill.
- In his gospel, Luke says Jesus was born "while Quirinius was governor of Syria" (Luke 2:2). But archaeological records showed that Quirinius left office five years earlier, before Herod was king—long before Jesus could have been born. "Aha!" crowed the skeptics. "Luke

goofed." But then they found another inscription. It seems Quirinius had two terms of office, and the second one corresponded with the time of Jesus' birth.

These are just a few examples. They don't prove that everything in the Bible is accurate, but they show that the Bible is serious history. We know more about Jesus than about Julius Caesar, more about Moses than about Plato. Historians don't doubt that Caesar was assassinated or that Plato wrote *The Republic*, even though they have to rely on very few ancient sources. The Bible itself is an ancient source that gives us valid history about the nation of Israel, history that has been verified in case after case.

So what happens when the Bible reports a miracle? If you assume that miracles can't happen, then you accuse those ancient writers of making things up. But why would they, when they were so careful about the rest of their reporting? Isn't it reasonable to allow for the possibility that miracles can happen, and that they could have happened at various points throughout the 2,000 years or so that the Bible describes?

"The second reason it makes sense to trust the Bible," says Dr. Moreland, "is *fulfilled prophecy*. Over and over again, the Bible predicts the future, hundreds of years before events happened. That's pretty unusual."

Example: The Book of Daniel describes a series of nations that would overrun Israel—and the Persians, Greeks, Syrians, and Romans fit those descriptions perfectly. Daniel even established a time frame for the appearance of the Messiah, one that fits the birth of Christ.

More examples: The prophet Micah said a Savior would be born in Bethlehem; Zechariah said He would ride in triumph into Jerusalem; Isaiah said He would suffer a criminal's death. Jesus fulfilled each of those prophecies. Psalm 22 gives a grotesquely precise picture of a crucifixion, though it was written centuries before the Romans invented that form of execution. Jesus Himself predicted the fall of Jerusalem to a Roman army, and that happened 40 years after Jesus died. There are even some amazing prophecies about the rebirth of the nation of Israel, which weren't fulfilled until 1948.

Skeptics say most of these "prophecies" were added later, after the "predicted" events happened. Or they say Jesus purposely fulfilled the prophecies about the Messiah. If you're sure that no one can ever predict the future, you have to adopt explanations like these. But what if there *is* a God who wants to give us "previews of coming attractions"? The number of biblical prophecies is so overwhelming that it's at least reasonable to consider the possibility.

"There is a third reason why a person should trust the Bible," says Dr. Moreland, "and it's that the Bible for thousands of years has *transformed cultures and people's lives* more than any other single book in the history of the world. I would challenge any person to come up with any book that is even close to rivaling the Bible in its impact."

This could be a dangerous point for Christians to make, because you have to take the bad with the good. Look around you at the people who believe the Bible. Are they people you want to be like? Some yes, some no. Throughout history, the Bible has had a phenomenal track record—civilizing Europe, establishing universities. Millions and millions of lives have been changed for the better by reading the Scriptures. On the other hand, some have misused the Bible to support the Crusades and slavery. But is that the Bible's fault?

The Bible's powerful impact might not prove that it's true. But it proves the Bible is important—and worth investigating for yourself. For resources to help you do that, see the "For Further Reading" list in the back of this book.

So where are we in our search for ultimate truth?

We've learned that feelings are helpful, but can be misleading.

We've seen that public opinion can be wrongheaded, though wise people can give us good guidance.

We've learned that thinking can get us far, but not far enough.

Where do we go from here?

We need information from another source, like the FBI hunting down the hackers. A source beyond our feelings, public opinion, and science. A source of ultimate truth.

Our feelings may tell us there has to be some God out there who knows the answers. Plenty of people believe in Him. It's reasonable to see His fingerprints all over creation. Now what?

We ask Him for more info.

That might sound crazy, but it makes a lot of sense.

If God gave us the ability to communicate, then He can probably communicate, too. If He made us with the ability to enjoy relationships, then He probably would want a relationship with us.

But if God wants to communicate with us, how would He do it?

The Bible claims to be the written answer to that question. From the Ten Commandments to the life and death and resurrection of Jesus, to the crazy dream John had in the Book of Revelation—the Bible presents itself as the truth of God.

Is it true because it says it's true? Of course not. But the Bible's claim to be God's Word raises some important questions. *Could* our Creator speak to us in a book like this? Absolutely. *Did* He? We need to read the book and see.

A few books, like the Bible, claim to be the ultimate truth. We need to weigh those claims. We can use our feelings, the wisdom of others, and our own reason to do it.

The *Book of Alphonse* will always come up short.

The Bible, however, is another story.

Eight

Back It Up

WELCOME TO TEENTALK
Screen Name: Tim4U
Logon 6:59 P.M.

butterfly:	No, I still see Carlos, too.
nobraner:	how do you feel about that?
butterfly:	OK, I think. And bad, too. I don't know.
Hulkster:	You're better off without him.
butterfly:	Maybe.
	[Tim4U has entered the chat room.]
nobraner:	where have you been, timbo? i've been waiting for you
Tim4U:	Uh-oh.
nobraner:	i have some questions
Hulkster:	Can the rest of us listen in, or is this a private matter?
nobraner:	it won't take long, but I'm desperate. i've been reading about jesus, and tim's the only christian i know.
wonderboy:	Well, the only one with a brain.
Tim4U:	Thanks, I think.

nobraner: i've been reading the book of john, like you said, and it's good. But there's this one part where jesus says, BEFORE ABRAHAM WAS BORN, I AM. is that a typo, or what?

Tim4U: Let me get my Bible. Just a sec.

butterfly: You're really serious about this stuff, aren't you? I used to be.

nobraner: what happened?

butterfly: Life, I guess.

wonderboy: No offense, but Christians are a bunch of hypocrites. I mean, they talk about Jesus and all, but they're just as bad as everyone else.

Hulkster: And they keep telling everyone else how to live.

nobraner: i just want to know about jesus, okay?

Tim4U: I'm back. You're in John chapter 8. About Abraham.

nobraner: but why does jesus say "i am"? abraham lived like hundreds of years before this, right?

Tim4U: That's the point. He's saying He's older than Abraham.

nobraner: but he wasn't, was he?

Tim4U: Not His earthly body. But He's saying He was around at the beginning.

Hulkster: This is so much fun.

butterfly: Wait! Wasn't "I AM" a name for God?

Tim4U: Yep.

butterfly: Sunday school pays off.

nobraner: so jesus is saying he's god?

Tim4U: Exactly. That's why people were so upset.

nobraner: bear with me guys, i have one more question

Tim4U: Shoot.

Hulkster:	Don't tempt me.
nobraner:	i got as far as chapter 14. jesus says, NO ONE COMES TO THE FATHER EXCEPT THROUGH ME.
Tim4U:	I'm looking it up. John 14:6.
nobraner:	is he saying that christianity is the only true religion?
Tim4U:	Well, yes.
Hulkster:	See, that's what I don't get. How can any one religion say it has all the answers?
butterfly:	It just doesn't seem like something Jesus would say.
wonderboy:	I agree. We have enough bigotry without one religion telling all the others they're wrong.
Tim4U:	I wish I could tell you that's not in the Bible, but it is.
nobraner:	but you still believe the bible?
Tim4U:	Yes. I've found it to be true in my life.
wonderboy:	But what about people who have found Buddhism true, or Muslimism?
Hulkster:	It's called Islam.
wonderboy:	Whatever. Can't they have the truth, too?
Tim4U:	I guess they can have truth IN them, but Jesus says He IS the truth.
nobraner:	what does that mean?
Tim4U:	I'm not sure.
Hulkster:	I just think everyone has the right to believe anything they want.
Tim4U:	They do, at least in this country.
Hulkster:	There are many ways to get to God. Lots of beliefs.

wonderboy:	Who's to say this religion is right and others are wrong?
Tim4U:	Maybe Jesus can say that.
nobraner:	looks like he did
wonderboy:	Nothing personal, Tim, but I think you Christians take this religion thing way too seriously.
Hulkster:	Yeah, lighten up a little. Let people be what they want.

REAL LIFE
The Common Grounds Coffee Shop with Tim (aka Tim4U)
Next Day

Tim Bennett ordered a cup of Jamaican Blue Mountain coffee at the counter, then found a high chair by the window while they brewed it. From this perch he viewed the passersby on this lazy Sunday afternoon, strolling the sidewalks of this sleepy town. He began to wonder what they believed . . . about God, about Jesus, about what was really important. His church had taught him to be concerned for their souls, but now a different lesson was brewing in his brain.

Let people be what they want.

He remembered that phrase, and others, from the chat room.

It made him look at the world with a different attitude. That cranky-looking couple—did they really want a relationship with God, or just a better marriage? Did that skateboarding kid want peace of mind, or a PlayStation 2?

Beth Bates, the church youth leader, appeared at the

door of the coffee shop. She pulled out the chair across from Tim and dumped her heavy canvas bag on the floor. "Did you order?"

"Jamaican Blue Mountain," Tim said, nodding. "Best stuff in the world."

"No way," she countered. "The cappuccino here is one of God's greatest creations."

The waitress came by with Tim's coffee. She was two years younger than Tim, with pretty eyes but a bad complexion. "Hi, Miss Bates," she chirped. "Can I get you anything?"

"Hi, Christine. I would love one of your cinnamon cappuccinos. And you can call me Beth."

"All right, Beth—coming right up." The girl whirled away and Beth settled into her seat.

"So, Tim, what's up? You said you had a question for me."

"Well, first of all, this isn't for me. It's for a . . . well, a friend of mine."

"Uh-huh."

"Really!" Tim knew that sounded phony, but he *was* trying to find a way to answer "nobraner" from the chat room. Yet the questions had been grating at him, too. "I'm not sure how to put it, but I've been wondering about—well, how do we know we're right?"

"What? About Christianity?"

"I mean, who's to say we're right and everyone else is wrong? Isn't it—I don't know—*rude* to say that Jesus is the only way? Why can't we just let people be what they want?"

Beth smiled. "Hold on there. I haven't had enough coffee yet to deal with all those questions at once." As if on cue, Christine came by with Beth's cappuccino.

"But do you see what I'm saying?"

"Yes, I get your drift." Beth fished her cell phone out of her purse. "What's your number?"

"What are you doing?"

"What's your number?"

He told her, and she started punching buttons. "All right. Here, you want to talk to your dad?"

Confused, Tim took the phone. After three rings a woman answered—no relation to Tim. In fact, she had a foreign accent. "Sorry," he muttered. "Wrong number."

"Oh, dear," said Beth, putting the phone away. "I thought I punched in all the numbers you said, but maybe not in the right order. Isn't it rude of the phone company to insist that you have to dial those numbers in that exact order? That's awfully narrow-minded, don't you think?"

"But that's the only way it works!"

"But who's to say that particular collection of numbers should be the only one that reaches your house?"

Tim thought a moment. "Well, the phone company says that. They came up with the system."

"Aha!" Beth exclaimed with a gleam in her eye. "So since they invented the system, they have the right to tell you how to get through."

It took a while, but Tim was finally getting it. "And God invented our system, so . . . so, what?"

"Look, Tim. We didn't make up Christianity. We're not telling anybody that we're smarter than they are. God put us here to begin with, and He's shown us how to get through to Him. Jesus is the One who makes that connection for us. But it's not that *we're* right and everyone else is wrong. *God* is right, and we're just listening to Him."

"But can't other ways be right, too?"

Beth took a sip of her cappuccino. "Well, they could be, if God said so. But He says that Jesus is the only way."

Tim was gazing out the window, at the people strolling the street. "But why can't there be many different ways?"

She carefully circled her coffee cup with her fingers. "All right. What's the best coffee in the world?"

"Jamaican Blue Mountain."

"You're wrong. It's cinnamon cappuccino."

"That's just your opinion," Tim argued.

"Exactly," Beth replied. "A lot of things in this world—like coffee flavors—are simply matters of taste. A lot of people think religion is the same way—a matter of flavor, not fact. If you're just making up ways to be a good person, maybe they're right. But if God is real, and He's already laid out His own plan, we'd better have the facts about what He's saying."

The conversation went on for another hour. Beth had some good ideas, Tim noticed, but she also knew when to shut up and let the other person talk. Along the way, she recommended some books: *Mere Christianity* by C.S. Lewis; *Evidence That Demands a Verdict* by Josh McDowell; and *How Now Shall We Live?* by Charles Colson. Beth even said he could borrow these books from her if he wanted.

As they gathered up cups and napkins, Beth looked out the window at the people Tim had been watching. "There are some good ideas in most religions. They can be right about a lot of things, and we don't have to be afraid to admit that. But God says there's one way to know Him personally, to get His power inside your life, and that's through Jesus.

"Is that narrow-minded to say? Maybe so. But if I'm in a burning building and someone says, 'Here, there's only one way out. Follow me!'—I'm not going to argue about how narrow-minded that is. We're all in a burning building, Tim, and we Christians are just pointing the way to safety."

AND NOW, BACK TO YOU . . .

What do the people you know seem to value most? Freedom, probably.

Maybe 50 years ago people were different, but today they "just got to be free." They're free to feel anything, think anything, say anything, and do . . . well, just about everything.

Freedom is generally a good thing. But it includes the freedom to be silly, to waste your life, and to do things that might harm you. It also includes the freedom to be wrong.

On a TV talk show recently, a man declared that he worshiped a different god—his pet mouse. Sure enough, there was the mouse scampering around the stage as the man described this newfangled religion. One of the other guests nearly stepped on this "god," but the host was careful about stepping on the man's feelings. After all, this man was free to choose any supreme being he wanted, even a little furry one.

Sure, maybe this guy was just grabbing his 15 minutes of fame, playing a big joke on the talk show audience. But for the sake of argument, let's assume he was absolutely sincere. Let's say he really felt a sense of devotion to this mouse.

Now here's the problem. He's free to have those feelings, but that doesn't mean those feelings are based on truth. Those are unreasonable feelings to have, quite frankly, and the rest of us ought to feel free to tell him that. (In fact, the studio audience was more critical than the host. They freely mocked the man's mouse-worship.)

But wait a minute! Who's to say that mouse-worship is for the birds? If this man gets a sense of purpose and well-being from honoring this rodent, what's wrong with that? Isn't his religion "true for him"?

That depends on your definition of religion. If religion is merely a tool for acquiring peace of mind, then hey . . . whatever gets you through the week. If religion is just a way to feel good about yourself, or a code of ethics to follow, or a way to express the worshipful feelings deep within your soul—then it's like flavors of coffee. You say cappuccino, I say espresso. There's no right or wrong about it. If you find something that works for you, go for it.

But if you expect religion to be a way to meet the living God, then you need to consider how *God* wants to meet *you*. You can't just make up any route you want. You have to pay attention to the map God is showing you.

Suddenly we've moved from flavors to facts. If God is offering Plan A, it doesn't matter how appealing Plans B through Z are. We need to go with God's plan.

"Who's to say what religion is right?" says Kay Coles James, a speaker and think tank member. "I'd ask God. I'd try to find out what God says."

It sounds so simple that people often overlook it. They assume that no one knows what God says, so we have to invent our own ways to reach Him—whether that's mouse worship or human sacrifice. But as noted in the previous chapter, it makes sense to believe that the God who created us as communicating beings wants to *communicate with us.* In that case, it's a matter of hearing what He says.

The question, says Talbot Seminary's Dr. J.P. Moreland, is this: "Is there any religion that has evidence that it was actually supernatural and wasn't just a human invention?"

"With Christianity," says Dr. Doug Geivett, who teaches philosophy at Biola University, "the idea is that God is speaking to us. God is breaking through the confusion and answering our questions with His solutions. But take any other religion and ask the same question."

Many religions don't even attempt to make this claim. Some do, but on shaky grounds. Yet, as Dr. Moreland observes, "Christianity provides evidence that it's actually true."

"All right," you might say, "but why does that have to mean other religions are false? You can have your Christian faith, but let others have their Muslim faith or Hindu faith or whatever. Why do Christians have to insist other beliefs aren't true? Isn't that just plain prejudice?"

First of all, let's understand that some *other religions have some wisdom in them.* Christians don't say that other faiths are all wrong all the time. Other beliefs have some good ethics, philosophies, and insights into the human condition.

But, second, we must recognize that there are also *major disagreements* on the basic questions: Who is God? Who is Jesus? How can we know God?

Many people assume that all religions are basically the same, like brands of toothpaste. But a closer look shows that's not true. Most religions claim that people earn a relationship with God through certain behavior or rituals. Christians claim that God has revealed a different way: Humans can't save themselves, and it takes the sacrifice of Jesus Christ, God in a body, to make the connection.

"[There are] a lot of religions out there," says youth speaker and author Dawson McAllister. "They can't all be right. They're saying opposite things."

For instance, a Christian believes that Jesus is the Son of God, the Messiah; a Jewish person may believe that Jesus was a good rabbi, but not the Messiah; a Muslim may believe that Jesus was a prophet of God (Allah), but not God. They can't all be right. Two plus two can't be four, five, *and* six. Either Jesus was God or He wasn't. If He wasn't, He wasn't a good rabbi or a good prophet, but a blaspheming liar.

"Don't give me this squishy 'Whatever's true to me is true to me,'" says McAllister. "In the end you have to say, 'I'm going to take a long look at this person Jesus Christ. I'm going to decide whether He told the truth or whether He's the most disgusting liar who ever lived.'"

That leads us to our third point. This "one way" stuff wasn't our idea. Christians didn't build a clubhouse and lock everyone out. *It was Jesus Himself who said He was the only way*: "I am the way and the truth and the life. No one comes to the Father except through me" (John 14:6). Even if we wanted to go with the flow and say, "Believe whatever you want, because it really doesn't matter," Jesus wouldn't let us. Oh, we could say that, but it wouldn't be Christianity. Jesus is the One who said, "Small is the gate and narrow the road that leads to life, and only a few find it" (Matthew 7:14).

Fourth, *Jesus backed up His claims by rising from the dead.* When it comes to evidence, here's the bombshell: Jesus died and came back to life.

Over the years, people have called this a myth, a hoax, or mass hysteria. But there are compelling reasons to believe it actually happened. And if it actually happened, then Jesus is more than just a man.

His tomb was empty. His body was gone. If the Roman or Jewish leaders could have produced the body, they would have; they wanted to put down this pesky faith. The disciples claimed to see Jesus alive after His death, to eat with Him, to touch Him—way too physical to be a hallucination. What's more, most of the disciples died for their belief in the resurrection. If they'd made it up, they surely would have changed their story at the point of Roman swords. But they stuck with their claim that Jesus rose from the dead.

The wisdom of Jesus' teachings is enough to make anyone sit up and take notice; many people of various religions honor Jesus as a wise teacher like Socrates or Confucius. Some affirm that He was a prophet or God-picked leader, like Moses or Muhammad or Martin Luther King, Jr. But the resurrection puts Jesus in a different league entirely. As the Apostle Paul put it, Jesus was "declared with power to be the Son of God by his resurrection from the dead" (Romans 1:4).

Does it still seem unfair, too narrow, to say that Christianity is the place to go for ultimate truth? Maybe one more observation will help: *Christians aren't trying to shut people out, but welcome them in.*

That may be hard to believe if you've known pushy Christians. But they aren't *supposed* to be that way. They're supposed to share truth because they want others to have the benefits of knowing God, too. If they hated people of other beliefs, they'd keep quiet about their own faith. *Love* is supposed to lead them to do otherwise.

"The truth is narrow, but the gift is for everyone," explains Dawson McAllister. That "John 3:16" that gets waved around at football games ought to be quoted in full every so often. It says that God loved the world so much that He gave His Son—Jesus—so that *whoever* believes in Him doesn't have to die apart from God but can have eternal life.

The gift is not just for a particular race or nation or clique, but for anyone who accepts it.

We're back to Beth's burning building. When a firefighter breaks through a window and says, "Here! Climb the ladder to safety," you don't say, "You're discriminating against people who want to take the stairs!" No, you're grateful for the way out.

According to Christianity, God is not cruel to offer only one way to be rescued. He's showing amazing love by offering that one way.

As for Christians, they don't mean to be arrogant by offering that pathway to others. In their imperfect way, they're trying to show love, too.

Nine

Enter Your Password

WELCOME TO TEENTALK
Screen Name: butterfly
Logon 9:18 P.M.

r2d2:   It's so weird. He is, like, losing it. In class he's like a zombie. He just lets us do our lab projects but doesn't say much. I've never seen a teacher like this before.

butterfly: And that's because he disagrees with the school board?

r2d2:   Not just that. His girlfriend left. She was also a teacher at the school.

butterfly: She quit?

r2d2:   Yes, and she moved out of town. I think they were having problems anyway, but he didn't expect this.

    [Tim4U has entered the chat room.]

butterfly: And I thought my life was a soap opera.

Tim4U: Hi, guys, what's up?

r2d2:   You don't want to know.

butterfly:	r2 has a teacher in self-destruct mode.
Tim4U:	Yikes!
wonderboy:	I'm going to ignore the fact that you just said Yikes.
Tim4U:	Sorry. Too many comic books.
r2d2:	Speaking of comic books, whatever happened to that girl with the Bible?
butterfly:	Yeah, nobraner hasn't been here for a week. I hope she's all right.
Tim4U:	She's OK. I've been e-mailing her.
wonderboy:	Oh, really??????
butterfly:	So you've been getting to know each other on the side, eh?
Tim4U:	Hate to disappoint you, but she just had some questions about the Bible.
wonderboy:	Yeah, right.
Tim4U:	Really. I recommended some books about what I believe.
r2d2:	I don't mean to be rude, but that's what I hate. Why can't you Christians keep your beliefs to yourself?
Tim4U:	She asked me questions. Was I supposed to ignore her?
r2d2:	Well, you got her started on the whole Christian thing, didn't you?
Tim4U:	Is it wrong to talk about what you believe?
r2d2:	Yes, if you're saying everyone else is wrong.
Tim4U:	Isn't that what you do with your scientific beliefs? Don't you say all the creationists are wrong? Aren't you trying to convince others that you're right?

wonderboy: Too-shay.

r2d2: Yeah, but that's scientific fact. It's a scientist's job to search for the truth and teach it to others. That's what Mr. Newson used to say.

butterfly: Isn't that everybody's job?

[nobraner has entered the chat room.]

butterfly: Welcome home, stranger. Where have you been?

nobraner: busy

wonderboy: Too busy for your pals in the chat room. :'(

nobraner: i was reading a lot, and thinking. needed to be by myself

butterfly: What were you reading?

nobraner: the bible

Tim4U: So, did you decide anything?

nobraner: yes, i did. i want to follow jesus

Tim4U: That's great!

butterfly: Wow, that's a big decision.

nobraner: i know

butterfly: I didn't think people really did that anymore.

Tim4U: What made you finally decide?

nobraner: well, i was fighting it. i was reading the bible and arguing in my head. then i finally said, what if it's true? when i stopped fighting, it started to make sense. i asked god to forgive the wrong stuff i've done and asked jesus to come into my life.

butterfly: That's nice, nb. I'm glad for you.

nobraner: i mean, i don't have all the answers . . . but i don't feel so empty. you know?

wonderboy: Whatever floats your boat.

r2d2:	Just don't start preaching at people and smiling all the time. And don't get big hair.
butterfly:	What's wrong with big hair?
r2d2:	All the Christians around here have big hair.
Tim4U:	To rest their halos on, probably. :)
r2d2:	Maybe it's different where you are.
wonderboy:	Here it's T-shirts. I thought the school had a big fishing club until I realized the fish was a Christian symbol.
r2d2:	They should have chosen the turkey instead.
wonderboy:	What I can't stand is when somebody in a Christian T-shirt is, like, cutting in line right in front of you. What hypocrites!
Tim4U:	Christians aren't perfect, just forgiven.
wonderboy:	That's the T-shirt this guy was wearing.
Tim4U:	But it's true!
r2d2:	Well, that's your opinion. And that's what you keep forgetting.
Tim4U:	What?
r2d2:	That you've got one point of view, but there are others.
nobraner:	look, i know people have other opinions, but i didn't accept jesus because i wanted big hair or t-shirts. it just became obvious to me that jesus was telling the truth
r2d2:	To YOU.
nobraner:	but if it's true, it's true. It's not my truth or your truth, but THE TRUTH!
wonderboy:	Whoa, baby! nobraner just used CAPITAL LETTERS AND AN EXCLAMATION POINT!
r2d2:	Hard to believe.

Tim4U: Isn't that a sign that the world is coming to an end?

nobraner: ha ha

REAL LIFE
At the School of Maria (aka butterfly)
Next Day

Maria sat in geometry tracing a triangle on her paper, over and over again.

"In a right triangle," the teacher was droning, "if we know the length of this side and the degrees of this angle, what do we know about this side and this angle? Anyone? Anyone?"

Of course William, the Bill Gates clone in the front row, would eventually answer, but only after everyone else in the room shrugged. Maria wasn't even shrugging. She just traced the triangle, pondering the angles of her life.

Jared-me-Carlos. Jared-me-Carlos. Her heart had been waging this war for months now. She'd broken up with bad boy Carlos three times, but he had sweet-talked her back to him. Jared was a constant, the right angle, always there for her, no matter how she treated him.

"Then according to our theorem," the teacher went on, "we know the angles add up to what? Anyone? Yes, 180— thank you, William. So in a right triangle, if this angle decreases, what happens to this angle? Anyone?"

Decrease, increase. Maria knew that feeling. Whenever her self-esteem decreased, her desire for Carlos increased. She lived a tough life, trying to get college-worthy grades while helping her single mom with her four younger brothers and sisters. Jared was an anchor, but when she got worn out, she was easily tempted.

"So according to the theorem of Pythagoras," the teacher continued, "if this side is x-squared and this side is y-squared, what is the hypotenuse?"

"A big, fat animal," said a voice from the back row. The near-comatose class snickered.

"Very funny," the teacher replied. "And I'd be laughing, too, if I hadn't heard it at least 10 TIMES EVERY YEAR FOR THE PAST 23 YEARS!" The class quieted as the teacher got a grip. "I know in this computer age you can just press a key and get all this figured out for you, but if you ever want to be the person *making* the computers rather than running to the shop every time yours breaks down, you need to learn this."

Front-row William was nodding vigorously. Maria kept tracing triangles, her thoughts drifting to last night's online chat. She'd always thought of the chat room as just a breather from the duties of each day, but something big had been happening there lately.

She had witnessed the changing of a life. Good old "nobraner," with depression so thick it could silence a sitcom laugh track, had grown interested in Jesus, read the Bible, and become a Christian. And that square-of-the-hypotenuse, "Tim4U," had helped her along the way.

Maria's pencil started a new triangle: "Tim4U" to "nobraner" to . . . "butterfly." The others didn't know it, but there was a third Christian in that chat room—Maria.

As a little girl, she'd stayed with her grandmother on weekends. Sundays they would attend a storefront church. She remembered the joy of raising her hands and waving them as they sang. One day her Sunday school teacher, a beautiful woman with a beautiful name—Mrs. Consuela Renalda Maria Martinez—asked her if she wanted to accept Jesus. She did. And in the next two years, her grandmother had taught her to follow Christ.

But then her grandmother died, and Maria plunged back into her mother's world, where no one had time for religion. By now, Jesus was a distant voice from down the block, a childhood portrait fading with time. She kind of missed the Jesus she had known as a girl, but she hadn't had much of a chance to think about Him lately.

Until now. "Tim4U," "nobraner," and "butterfly"—a triangle of faith. The Christian, the newcomer, and the buried treasure. What would it take, Maria wondered, to dig up that faith of hers? Could she ever become a real Christian again?

"I know you think these are just a bunch of old laws invented by the ancient Greeks," the teacher was saying, "but don't you see? Everything comes down to triangles. Vectors, trajectories—it's all triangles—and that's what sends spaceships to Mars!"

But Maria was still putting together triangles of her own. *Jesus, me, and . . . and what? My life. If Jesus is the right angle, the constant, and I increase the angle of my commitment, what does the other side look like?*

She frowned. What did the other side look like *now?* She wasn't a bad girl, was she? She worked hard and treated people well, with the possible exception of her sister Sara. And Maria wasn't a party girl. She'd seen the damage done to some of her best friends by drugs and drinking, so she stayed clean—pretty much.

Didn't her life look pretty Christian already? Except

maybe for the thing with Carlos and Jared. And she'd probably have to go to church somewhere. *But besides that, I
wouldn't have to change much.*

Her eyes fell on the first triangle she'd drawn in class that
day. The flowery "M" on one side for Maria. The block-lettered
"J" for Jared. And the "C" with flames erupting around it. *Oh,
no,* she thought. *I guess Carlos has to go for good.*

She knew he was all wrong for her. Every good thing in her
life, he put down. Every wicked spark, he fanned. If she truly
wanted to live as a Christian, she knew she had to say no to
Carlos once and for all. Maybe this time Jesus would help her.

Her eyes focused on the stone-solid "J" in front of her.
Jared was a great guy, probably too good for her. Her family
loved him, her friends wanted him, and he put up with her
shaky moods. What more could she want? She doodled some
vertical stripes in and around the big, blocky "J." It looked all
too appropriate: prison bars. When Maria was with Jared,
she felt trapped, smothered. It was like they were married
already, and she didn't want that. Maybe that was why she
kept running back to Carlos. As bad as he was, he offered a
kind of freedom.

The teacher kept droning and Maria kept doodling. The
"J" became JESUS, with the "C" curving into the final "S."
Both those letters became wings, with the prison bars
transforming into crosshatched designs. The triangles
spawned other triangles, connecting until Maria's whole
paper was filled with the glorious image of a butterfly in
flight.

Finally the bell rang, and the class swarmed out. In slow
motion Maria placed her drawing in her notebook and
began to shuffle toward the door. The teacher, slumped

against the chalkboard, said wearily, "Maria, you're usually more attentive. Did you learn *anything* in class today?"

"Sure," she answered brightly. "It made a lot of things very clear to me. About triangles."

That evening, Maria decided, she would go over and break things off with Carlos once and for all. She knew it wouldn't be easy, but she said a little prayer for help. *Jesus, remember me? Look, if You want me to do this, You gotta help me. Please!*

She called Carlos to make sure he'd be home. He must have sensed something was wrong, because he turned on more charm than usual. "Baby, you mean everything to me. You know that? I can't wait to see you." He said he had to help his brother with something, but he'd be home by six.

Maria practiced her breakup speech all afternoon, doing her chores, and on the bus over to Carlos's block. She sent a few more prayers heavenward. It was about 5:45 when she got there, so she camped out at the corner pizza place, bought a Pepsi, and tried to fend off her second thoughts. *Jesus, I know when I look in his eyes, I'll lose my nerve. You gotta help me.*

That's when it happened.

Maria caught a glimpse of Carlos walking past the pizza place. She grabbed her half-empty cup of Pepsi and ran to catch him. Even then her will was weakening. But as she got outside, she saw he was walking with another girl, his arm around her.

The paper cup, weighted with Pepsi and crushed ice, hit him on the back of the head, splattering both Carlos and his new gal pal.

Carlos yelled, trying to explain things over the curses of

the girl next to him. Across the street some kids on bikes stopped to watch the show. A few patrons stepped outside the pizza place to see the action.

Just as Maria was proclaiming that she never wanted to see Carlos again, and that she was crazy for ever seeing him at all, she saw a familiar form step out of one of the homes along the block. It was Jared.

Maria crumpled to the sidewalk in tears. Carlos ran after his new girl. Jared slowly walked toward Maria, stepping over the paper cup. "They told me about you and Carlos," he said, "but I didn't believe them. Now . . . well, I think we're through now."

Over the next few days, Jared wouldn't take her calls. When he finally did, his voice was icy. They were history.

Maria scolded Jesus for making things turn out so badly. "I wanted to be a Christian again, and this is how You treat me?" She stayed out of the chat room for a while, not sure if she could deal with the Christians there—or the non-Christians. She felt as if she were somewhere in-between.

Then one day at her locker she dropped her notebook. Some papers spilled out. She saw the elaborate butterfly she'd doodled in geometry. There, stretching from wing to wing, was the name of the One who, she had to admit, had set her free from the triangles that had trapped her.

J-E-S-U-S.

AND NOW, BACK TO YOU . . .

Imagine you're attending a wedding. The church is festooned with flowers; families and friends gather in their sharpest attire to witness the vows. The bride, swathed in white, marches majestically down the aisle to meet her grinning groom. They repeat their vows solemnly.

Then, just before the "I do," the groom says, "Of course, we can still date other people, right?"

Wrong! That's the whole point of a marriage—"forsaking" all others and committing yourself to that one special person. Sure, some people start worrying about all the gallivanting they're giving up. But the emphasis of a wedding is on what the bride and groom are *gaining*.

A couple in love isn't thinking about dating other people. Faith in Jesus is like that. It's a loving commitment to be true to one Lord and one Lord only. As in a marriage, you "forsake all others"—but the emphasis is on what you're gaining, a real relationship with a powerful God who loves you like crazy.

Is it narrow-minded for Jesus to want our undivided loyalty? That's what He asks for, after all. He said things like these:

> "No one can serve two masters. Either he will hate the one and love the other, or he will be devoted to the one and despise the other" (Matthew 6:24).
> "If you love me, you will obey what I command" (John 14:15).
> "Greater love has no one than this, that he lay down his life for his friends. You are my friends if you do what I command" (John 15:13-14).

Jesus wants a committed relationship. He promises to love us so well, we won't need to go looking for anyone else.

Here's a dumb thing that people say: "I looked all over for my keys, and wouldn't you know it? They were in the last place I looked." *Of course* they were in the last place you looked. Why would you keep looking after you've found them?

The same thing is true of a relationship with Jesus. Once we find ultimate truth in knowing Him, we can stop overturning every rock in the hope of finding something to hold onto. We should keep looking *into* the truth of Jesus, but we don't need to hunt anywhere else for the answers to our deepest longings.

So why do people like "butterfly" find it hard to settle down with Jesus and keep looking to Him for the truth they need?

Again, it's like marriage. Some marriages don't last. As lovey-dovey as the bride and groom are on their wedding day, they might be helter-skelter within a few years. One or both start looking elsewhere for "true love."

Maybe they get *tempted*. They undervalue what they have and overvalue what they don't. The Astroturf looks greener on the other side of the field.

Maybe they get *lazy*. Any commitment takes work. Love may feel great, but it also takes effort. You have to do what it takes to please the one you love.

A relationship with God is the same way. Once we find ultimate truth in Jesus, we may feel great. But *living* the truth takes work.

Maria found that out. Temptation—aka Carlos and Jared—offered her a great new "adventure" while putting down what she already had. It got easier and easier to excuse herself from having to deal with all those no-compromise truths Jesus taught.

Maria's not alone. Many people like the idea of belonging to Jesus, going to heaven, that sort of thing. But they'd rather forget that the One who *is* truth has laid out some truths He wants followed. Sure, they're for our own good—but they're true because *He's* the truth, not just because they make our lives work better.

That brings us to the cutting-edge question Maria was beginning to consider. In a loving relationship with Jesus, how does He want us to live? If God is ultimate truth, and His instructions in the Bible don't match the way we're living, what should change?

We should. And we can, with His help.

It might mean re-evaluating our relationships, figuring out which friends (and boyfriends or girlfriends) support us in living truthfully. It might mean reconsidering our activities—measuring them against guidelines in the Bible.

Maria found that her relationships with Carlos and Jared didn't measure up. She had to let them go. It was a hard choice, and she would have preferred a quieter, less messy way to make it. In time, though, she began to see the benefits.

You might not experience the street-corner fireworks Maria saw. But God *will* help you live the truth, if you ask Him.

Ten

Now Connecting

WELCOME TO TEENTALK
Screen Name: nobraner
Logon 7:53 P.M.

nobraner:	met with my guidance counselor today
wonderboy:	You need guidance?
nobraner:	actually, yes
r2d2:	I don't think I've ever seen my guidance counselor.
nobraner:	same here. she didn't know my name. kept calling me janice
wonderboy:	Instead of "nobraner."
nobraner:	no, julie. that's my name.
butterfly:	Oh, I'm Maria.
wonderboy:	Greg here.
r2d2:	Rob.
	[Hulkster has just entered the chat room.]
butterfly:	Yo, Hulk, what's your name?
Hulkster:	Hulk.
wonderboy:	No, your real name.
Hulkster:	Hulk.

r2d2: And you're six-foot-three and you smash boulders.

Hulkster: Okay, so my girlfriend called me Mike. Why am I the center of attention?

r2d2: We're just talking about names.

wonderboy: And guidance.

butterfly: So, Julie, what kind of guidance did you need?

r2d2: From your name-impaired guidance counselor.

Hulkster: Who's Julie?

nobraner: me. it was about college.

Hulkster: I don't think I HAVE a guidance counselor.

r2d2: You do, but you have to break the law to get an appointment.

butterfly: So you're going to college?

nobraner: i hope so. but i have no clue where.

r2d2: Join the club. I've got 20 colleges sending me stuff and I'm just a junior.

butterfly: Must be nice.

nobraner: well, i'm a senior and i haven't even started looking

wonderboy: Can you say community college?

nobraner: my grades are good enough for a pretty good school

butterfly: So what's the problem?

nobraner: this is like a really important decision and i don't know what to do

wonderboy: What field do you want to go into?

nobraner: i don't know. that's part of the problem.

r2d2: What does the Bible say about it?

nobraner:	what?
r2d2:	You're reading the Bible now, right? That's supposed to give you the truth, right?
nobraner:	yeah, i guess
r2d2:	So what truth does it give you about choosing a college? I mean, if it's supposed to be God's Word, like you say, shouldn't God tell you what to do?
nobraner:	i never thought about that
butterfly:	Good idea, though.
wonderboy:	You're kidding.
nobraner:	i don't know that god has like ONE place he wants me to go
r2d2:	Why not? Isn't there one absolute truth about that? Isn't there a right or wrong about what college to attend?
nobraner:	i don't know. i'm new at this
wonderboy:	The Bible is just a bunch of stories. It can't tell you what to do.
Hulkster:	Yeah, when people run their lives by the Bible, they start handling snakes and seeing UFOs.
wonderboy:	No, that's when they start running their lives by the X-Files.
Hulkster:	Sorry. I get them mixed up.
butterfly:	I think the Bible has a lot to say about how to live.
Hulkster:	Maybe in a general way, but not picking a college.
r2d2:	They didn't even HAVE colleges then. You want nice sayings, try the Bible. You want to make decisions, you're on your own.

wonderboy:	Maybe you should call the Psychic Friends Hotline.
nobraner:	I've been reading the bible a lot, and it's like god speaks to me there
r2d2:	Uh-oh. What does he "say"?
nobraner:	encouragement, mostly. but sometimes he challenges me to change.
r2d2:	Change how?
nobraner:	like put up with my parents
r2d2:	Then why can't he tell you where to go to college?
wonderboy:	Looks like this absolute truth deal isn't all it's cracked up to be.
r2d2:	Not the most useful thing in the world. What are you supposed to do with it?
Hulkster:	It slices. It dices.
nobraner:	like i said, i'm new at this.

REAL LIFE
Home of Julie (aka nobraner)
That Night

With a final click of the mouse, Julie signed off the Net. Frowning at the screen, she thought about the jabs of "r2d2" and "wonderboy." What good *was* it to know the "truth" if it didn't help you with the specific, everyday decisions of life?

Not that the Bible hadn't given her *any* guidance so far. In the two weeks since deciding to become a Christian, she'd read the Book every night—sometimes even in the afternoon. She'd prayed before and after each reading. She'd tried to follow some of Jesus' teaching, like, "Do to others as you would have them do to you" (Luke 6:31).

She snickered softly. Now *that* had been an interesting day, the day she'd tried to live out that Golden Rule verse. *Okay*, she'd told herself. *Today, for one whole day, I'll think about the way I treat other people.* And she'd done it, more or less. The verse had become a lens through which she viewed everything at school. She'd even stopped herself from making a cutting remark about a classmate's hair. *If Becky Seifert wants to make a nest for lost birds on top of her head,* Julie had thought, *that's her business. But I don't need to say anything about it out loud.*

The Golden Rule experiment had been tougher *after* school, though. Her mother had gotten home for dinner that night, just in time to nuke some frozen fish and broccoli. Then, for 27 agonizing minutes, mother and daughter had sat across the dinner table from each other, trying to manufacture conversation.

"How are your classes?"

"All right."

"Getting good grades?"

"A's and B's."

"Do you like your teachers?"

"They're okay."

Mom had been like a guidance counselor, trying to catch up with a girl she'd been ignoring. Then things had taken a turn for the worse.

"Are you still in . . . that cult?" Mom had asked.

"Mom, it's not a cult." Julie had felt all her muscles tense. *Do unto others,* she kept reminding herself. *Treat Mom the way you wish she'd treat you.*

Julie had taken a deep breath, then dived in. "Mom, I'm going through a lot of changes lately—but they're good changes. Someday I'll tell you about it all, but I don't think I'm ready yet."

Mom had looked up doubtfully from the overcooked bits of brown and green that littered her plate. "Changes?"

"I've—I've just found a new way to live, a kind of guide for my life. It's changing me. I used to feel really empty all the time, but now it's like there's something to live for."

Her mother had sighed deeply. "It *is* a cult. I saw something like this on *60 Minutes* once."

Julie had felt her jaw clench. She wanted to revert to her old sarcasm and crack, "Sure, Mom, it's a cult! We're all going to move into a compound on the planet Jupiter!" But then she remembered the *Do unto others,* and for once she didn't feel like slamming doors. Maybe she really *was* changing.

She had stared downward at her empty plate, gathering her thoughts, then spoken slowly and logically. "What cult gives a daughter back to her mother? Cults take people away and tell lies about everyone else. But I'm following Jesus. I think He's teaching me how to love. How to love *you.* But it's hard sometimes."

And she had walked upstairs, leaving her mother open-mouthed.

Now, sitting in front of the computer, Julie felt less confident about it all.

She turned off the computer and got ready for bed, thoughts of college and guidance and truth colliding in her head. She opened the Bible, the same red leather-bound one Sheri had lent her, to the place marked by the scarlet ribbon.

Romans, chapter 12. She remembered feeling really confused about the previous night's reading. *I hope chapter 12 makes more sense. And I hope it tells me which college to go to.*

"Therefore, I urge you, brothers, in view of God's mercy, to offer your bodies as living sacrifices, holy and pleasing to God—this is your spiritual act of worship" (Romans 12:1). *Living sacrifices?* She'd seen enough bad movies about lost tribes living near volcanoes to know that human sacrifices *died*—that was the whole point. So what was a *living* sacrifice? She read the next verse.

"Do not conform any longer to the pattern of this world, but be transformed by the renewing of your mind. Then you will be able to test and approve what God's will is—his good, pleasing and perfect will."

God's will—she'd heard Sheri use those words easily, as if they described a brand of toothpaste. But what was it? Whatever God wanted, right? Even about things like which college to go to?

Hmmmm. So you find out the truth about what God wants by . . . being transformed.

For a moment she felt confused, but then she remembered the year when all the little boys on the block suddenly had these robots that transformed into cars and spaceships. Transformers, they were called, because they changed from one thing into another. Now *she* was supposed to be the transformer, or the transformee. This involved the "renewing" of her mind. Maybe that was like renewing a magazine subscription, she thought. Making something new again.

She sighed. This was getting heavy, and she was getting thirsty. She padded downstairs to get a drink of water, tiptoeing past the TV room, where Mom was watching Leno.

Julie just wanted to grab a glass and get back upstairs before her mother noticed. She didn't want a conversation.

She would have made it, too, if it weren't for a little voice in her head. Not somebody talking, exactly, but a thought that didn't seem to come from her. A new thought.

Talk to her, it said.

But I don't like to talk to her, Julie thought.

But you're changing, said the voice. *Transforming.*

A shudder ran down her spine, and all at once she knew what she needed to do. She felt herself stepping into the TV room and heard herself saying, "Mom, can I talk to you?"

Startled, her mother looked up from Leno's monologue.

"I need some advice," Julie said. It still didn't feel natural, but she said it anyway.

Her mother's eyes grew wide with surprise, and the woman hit the POWER button on the remote. There was a small, crinkly sound from the TV as the screen went black.

"I . . . need some help figuring out where to go to college," Julie said. Then she sighed.

This wasn't going to be easy. But then change never was.

AND NOW, BACK TO YOU . . .

There's a show on TV that features what might seem to be the ideal situation: a bunch of attractive young people in a house with video cameras in every corner. And no rules!

But an odd thing happens in this "perfect" setting. People get on one another's nerves. They leave the cap off the toothpaste or the toilet unflushed. They make noise when others are trying to sleep. They invite friends to dinner without telling anyone.

How do they deal with these problems?

They make rules.

Even if we don't *like* rules and guidelines, we have to accept that they're necessary. Why? Because people often go too far.

So where should we get our rules? What guidelines are ultimately true?

Let's answer that question with a question. When you lug a new Hewlett-Packard computer home from the store, do you dig out an old Radio Shack manual to tell you how to set it up? No, the maker gives you instructions for the setup and maintenance of your machine. It makes sense to believe that *our* Maker has done the same thing.

We've already seen that it's reasonable to believe that we *have* a Maker, that He wants to communicate with us, sharing the truth about Himself. We've seen that it's reasonable to believe that Jesus Christ embodies this truth, and that the Bible is a one-of-a-kind truth source.

But how do we make the connection between the "big truths" of the Bible and the "little truths" we need to make everyday choices? What's the "truth" about how to treat your younger sister when she feeds your earrings to the dog? What's the "truth" about what you should say when your best friend asks, "Do I look fat?" What's the "truth" about which summer job to take, or who you should marry?

The Bible *does* provide guidelines for living. Long before that TV show demonstrated that people need help to get along, God was coming up with "road rules" for those who want to live His way. That's why the Bible has a lot to say about things like lying, killing, and stealing.

But does it say anything specifically about toothpaste caps? Or where to go to college?

The case of Julie can shed some light on this subject. Since she's decided to follow Jesus, a change is happening inside her. She didn't used to care what God thought about anything, but now she does. She reads the Bible, looking for truth. She prays, asking God questions. She listens, in case He wants to guide her thinking.

Will God tell her which college to attend? Will the "right" college brochure fall from the sky? Will she discover a verse that names her future alma mater?

Probably not. Those things may not be impossible, but they don't happen very often.

Here's what *does* seem to be happening in Julie's case. As she puts into practice the Bible's guideline to treat others the way she'd like to be treated, the barriers between her and her mom begin to come down. She goes to Mom for advice about college—and Mom may actually have some good ideas.

The process doesn't stop there, though. As she thinks about college, Julie may be able to set priorities based on more of God's guidelines.

For instance, she may come across other pieces of truth in the Bible, like Ephesians 5:18: "Do not get drunk on wine, which leads to debauchery. Instead, be filled with the Spirit." That may lead her to avoid a "party" school, because drinking heavily at frat bashes isn't very important to her anymore.

If she keeps reading the New Testament and reaches the

Book of James, she'll find more to chew on. On the subject of making choices, she'll see this tip: "If any of you lacks wisdom, he should ask God, who gives generously to all without finding fault, and it will be given to him. But when he asks, he must believe and not doubt, because he who doubts is like a wave of the sea, blown and tossed by the wind. That man should not think he will receive anything from the Lord; he is a double-minded man, unstable in all he does" (1:5-8).

Later in James she may read, "But the one who is rich should take pride in his low position, because he will pass away like a wild flower" (1:10). This might cause her to rethink her desire for a "status" school that would get her a high-paying job, because money isn't her main priority. She may even consider majoring in a people-helping field when she gets to verse 27 in the same chapter: "Religion that God our Father accepts as pure and faultless is this: to look after orphans and widows in their distress and to keep oneself from being polluted by the world."

Julie doesn't have to throw a bunch of college catalogs down the front steps and pray that the "right" one lands on top. Instead, she needs to let God transform her priorities and help her make decisions based on what's important to her—and to Him. That transformation happens as she gets to know God better, as she discovers more truth in His Book, and as she practices what she learns.

Julie's learning to listen—and to change. When it comes to applying ultimate truth to everyday choices, those are the first steps on a lifelong journey.

Eleven
Think Different?

WELCOME TO TEENTALK
Screen Name: Tim4U
Logon 8:07 P.M.

wonderboy:	Saw a great movie over the weekend.
butterfly:	Yeah? What?
wonderboy:	College a la Mode.
butterfly:	I saw that a week ago.
Hulkster:	Me too. Really funny.
r2d2:	It was dumb.
Hulkster:	So?
wonderboy:	You have to admit it was hilarious.
r2d2:	In a dumb sort of way.
Hulkster:	That scene with the ice cream cone was priceless.
butterfly:	I couldn't believe they did that.
Tim4U:	What was that rated?
wonderboy:	Who cares?
Tim4U:	Just wondering.
Hulkster:	You mean you didn't see it?
Tim4U:	Doesn't sound like something I'd like.

wonderboy:	How do you know if you haven't seen it?
Tim4U:	I think I got the gist of it.
r2d2:	Sex.
Tim4U:	Right. I don't think I'm going to see it.
wonderboy:	Why not?
Tim4U:	It's just about sex!
wonderboy:	I just checked. It's rated PG-13. You are 13, aren't you?
Tim4U:	Ha ha.
wonderboy:	Well, sometimes I wonder.
Hulkster:	You don't think about sex?
Tim4U:	I just choose not to focus on it, OK?
wonderboy:	It's a religious thing, right? Maybe you Christians want to pretend that sex doesn't exist, but I've got news for you.
Tim4U:	I'm just saying sex isn't a joke. And it's just for people who are married.
r2d2:	Married?
Hulkster:	Are you for real?
Tim4U:	God says sex should be reserved for marriage.
r2d2:	Maybe YOUR God says that.
Tim4U:	I didn't make this up. The Bible says it.
Hulkster:	So?
r2d2:	I know what it is. You're gay, aren't you?
Tim4U:	No!
r2d2:	Not that there's anything wrong with that.
Tim4U:	Well, now that you mention it . . .
wonderboy:	Oh, so you hate gay people too.
Tim4U:	I don't hate gay people.

r2d2:	Then homosexuality is OK? I knew you were in the closet!
Tim4U:	No!
butterfly:	No to what? OK or closet?
Tim4U:	Both! I'm not gay, and that kind of sex is not OK.
Hulkster:	Hey, that rhymes.
wonderboy:	It would make a great rap song.
Hulkster:	I don't think so, homey.
wonderboy:	Did you call me honey?
Hulkster:	No!
r2d2:	Explain yourself, Tim.
Tim4U:	You're just going to crucify me on this point, too.
butterfly:	No, Tim. Tell us what you think.
Tim4U:	It's not what I think. It's what God thinks.
r2d2:	What YOUR God thinks. Or what you THINK he thinks.
Tim4U:	What He says in the Bible.
butterfly:	But isn't that a matter of interpretation?
Tim4U:	No, it's pretty clear. God loves everybody, but He puts certain kinds of sexual activity out of bounds.
wonderboy:	No offense, but you're hopeless. Only bigots are against being gay now.
butterfly:	I have a friend who's gay, and he's the most caring person I've ever known.
wonderboy:	So what do you say to that, Timmy?
r2d2:	Timmy the Intolerant.
Tim4U:	I knew I should have stayed in bed this morning.

REAL LIFE
On the Way to School with Tim (aka Tim4U)
Next Morning

Tim squinted at the sunshine as he trudged toward school. There was a dull ache behind his eyes. He didn't want to keep thinking about last night's computer conversation, but he couldn't seem to help it.

Once they'd brought up homosexuality, things had gone from bad to worse. The more he'd tried to explain what he believed, the more he was branded as a narrow-minded jerk who wanted to force his morality on everybody else. He'd tried to explain that these weren't just his own opinions, that he was following what God said in the Bible—but that just got him into more trouble.

He'd been tempted to log off, but felt a certain duty to hang in there. After all, if God's Word was absolutely true, shouldn't everyone know that? After a half hour or so of wrangling, the subject drifted back to movies—less controversial ones. Tim eventually clicked out of the conversation.

Now, walking toward school, he could still see the other kids' angry words on the screen of his mind. What had he done wrong? He was just trying to tell the truth. He thought he'd been polite. Why did everyone think he was a bigot?

Maybe I should just keep quiet about my beliefs, he thought.

Just then his concentration was jarred by voices from two guys ahead of him.

"You don't know nothin'!" one was saying. "Michael Jordan was the best ever."

"No, Chamberlain was better," the other responded. "He had the skills."

"That is so slim. Michael was king for, like, ever. What did the Stilt ever do?"

"You see that man *jump*? He had wings."

"You are so absent. Get an angle."

As Tim neared the school, he saw streams of students gathering from all directions. He caught bits of chatter along the way:

"It's a shame about Mindy's hair. That color is so twenti-eth century."

"It was the greatest concert, man. I couldn't hear any-thing for two days."

"New tattoo? It rocks. I wanna get, like, a lion on my back, but my dad would shoot me."

"Why are you applying there? That's a jock school."

Tim sighed. Everybody seemed to be sharing nothing *but* opinions. Why couldn't *he*?

First period was Modern Life class. It was the school's way of being "on the edge" in education, letting kids clip newspapers and swap opinions. Every Monday was Five-for-Five Report Day, when five students gave five-minute talks on things they'd read in the Sunday paper.

On this day Adrian Lipscomb was talking about a recent court ruling on abortion. "I think every woman ought to have a right to make a free choice, and this 48-hour waiting period is just a way to keep her from making that choice. If she decides to have an abortion, well, she's already made up her mind, so why should she have to wait? It's her body."

Tim frowned, but kept quiet. He thought the waiting

period would help some women make *better* choices. But he didn't want to be labeled as a bigot.

It seemed to go that way throughout the morning. In history, Mr. Howard said that, in his opinion, Napoleon was the greatest military leader of all time. In physics, Miss Chen predicted that, in her opinion, there would be a workable unified field theory within 10 years.

At lunch, half the kids at Tim's table were arguing over which fast-food place had the best fries. Dani Foster was telling Amy Krupp she should get her astrological charts done. Joey Wetzel was campaigning for his girlfriend, explaining why she'd be the best prom queen.

All day long, people freely expressed their opinions. They said what they thought, and others let them. Even when there was disagreement, everyone seemed to accept that each person had a right to an opinion.

So why did Tim's opinions about Christianity make him a target of abuse? Why couldn't he express his beliefs without setting off a hail of criticism?

He thought about that on the way home, when he stopped at Common Grounds for a cup of coffee. Grabbing a table in back, he tried to think like "wonderboy," "Hulkster," and "r2d2." What was their problem with his beliefs? If he'd claimed that "the healing power of crystals" had given him a new lease on life, would they have launched their complaints with the same force?

Probably not. So what's the trouble?

His chat room comrades seemed most upset when Tim's beliefs conflicted with other people's behavior. They didn't like it when he said that certain kinds of sexual activity were wrong. Apparently it was okay to have an opinion as long as you didn't claim anyone else was wrong.

But how does that work? he thought. The people at lunch who said Wendy's had the best fries—weren't they saying the Burger King fans were wrong? Wasn't Dani, the amateur astrologer, implying that Amy's life was inadequate without guidance from the stars? When Joey said that his girlfriend, Crystal, would be the best prom queen, wasn't he knocking every other contestant?

Duh, Tim thought. *When you express an opinion, you're saying that conflicting opinions are wrong. You can't have both Wilt and Michael as the best B-ball player of all time. Choose one.*

Tim had chosen. He'd chosen to believe that God speaks through the Bible, and that there are certain ways God wants people to live. Then he'd dared to tell others about his choice. Shouldn't he have the right to be heard?

Tim looked up from his coffee. There, near the door, was the girl they called Crazy Alice. *Oh, no,* he thought, but fought the urge to run and hide. Alice had ADD or bipolar disorder or something and often forgot to take her medication, so you never knew what she might say. Most other kids avoided her, but Tim had tried to be nice to her.

She found her way to Tim's table, then stood in front of him. She went on and on about something she'd seen on the SciFi Channel the night before. "I think there are alien beings circling the earth right now," she said, leaning forward a bit too far and looking Tim in the eye. "They're just like us, Tim, only completely different. And they send beams into our minds and make us do things we don't want to do."

Tim traced squares on the table with his finger, half listening. Alice talked nonstop.

"They're from Pluto, I think, or Neptune maybe, and they're taking control. But you can stop them if you do your times tables backwards. Then they can't calibrate their wavelengths. Ready? Nine times nine is eighty-one. . . ."

Finally Tim lost it. "Look, Alice, that's just . . . well, it's crazy. I'm sorry, but someone has to tell you!"

Alice stared at him, her mouth half open.

"I've been listening to people express their opinions all day!" Tim protested. "I've kept quiet, but this is too much!" The other coffee drinkers looked up from their brews to see who was making so much noise, but Tim didn't care. "People can say whatever they want about whatever they think, and it's okay. Aliens? Astrology? Sure! But when I try to share *my* beliefs, I'm a bad guy, a hypocrite, a nut. I just don't get it!"

A big smile crept across Alice's face. All at once Tim knew he'd been duped.

"Gotcha," Alice said softly, and giggled.

Tim slumped over his coffee cup. "I give up," he groaned.

AND NOW, BACK TO YOU . . .

If your classmates are thinking about sex every 8.3 seconds, and you come along and say sex ought to be reserved for marriage, how do you expect them to respond?

If the unwritten student body motto is "Cheat if you can get away with it," and you dare to write a letter to the school paper that says otherwise, will it make you more popular?

If you express an opinion about homosexuality or abortion or caring for the poor, and base it on a 1,900-year-old book that you claim is the Word of God, will most people cheer you on?

No. They'll just think you've got a problem.

And what problem is that? If you're a Christian, they may think your "odd" ideas are rooted in causes like these:

Christians are ignorant. Many people, especially those like "r2d2," assume that believers in God-given truth just don't know any better. If Christians really knew the facts about evolution or philosophy or even the Bible, the reasoning goes, they would have a more "mature" view of life.

Christians are stuck in time. Some people think Christians never made it into the twentieth century, much less the twenty-first. Bible-believers supposedly long for the "good old days" and oppose any modern advances.

Christians are afraid to really live. According to this view, those who believe in ultimate truth just can't let loose. They're afraid of sex, new ideas, and anything not specifically okayed in the Bible. Sometimes people try "reverse evangelism" on Christians, trying to get them to conquer their fear of fun, let their hair down, and *party.*

Christians feel guilty about everything. Some psychologists—and even friends—think they need to help Christians get rid of that pesky sense of right and wrong. These "helpers" think the problem is merely guilty *feelings*—when the Bible says that sometimes people *are* guilty because they've done wrong.

Christians hate people who aren't like them. If you oppose certain behaviors and disagree with certain beliefs, many people assume you hate those who practice those behaviors and hold those beliefs. If you say the Bible calls homosexual activity a sin, many people assume you hate homosexuals. If you pray for the conversion of Muslims or Buddhists, people think you're dissing those groups.

Christians don't want anyone to have fun. Urging people to observe certain limits on things like sex and drinking earns you the title of "party pooper."

Christians want to control what everyone does and thinks. Especially when Christians become active politically, others can get the idea that anyone who believes in absolute truth is a control freak who wants to force nonbelievers to toe the line.

Christians think they know it all. If you believe you know the truth about something and sound really sure of yourself, people may think you're proud of yourself—as if you made this "truth" up.

Where does that leave you? If you believe in ultimate truth, how can you communicate it in a world that doesn't want to hear it?

Very carefully.

To start with, check those eight misunderstandings listed above. Sometimes Christians *earn* them. After all, Christians *can* be ignorant or stuck in time. They *can* be afraid to live a full life, or feel guilty about things that God's already forgiven them for. Sometimes they *do* show hatred for other people, want to control others, or think they know it all. Try asking yourself: *Do any of these descriptions sound like me?*

Then consider the following pointers.

Relationship first. It's possible to lose a friend by winning an argument. It's not your job alone to convince people of God's truth; His Holy Spirit can do that. This doesn't mean that you should approve of or participate in stuff that God considers sinful, but you don't need to be scolding people all the time. Love people even when you disagree with them. Take time to listen to them, help them, pray for them. If they ask your opinion, give it—gently. Remember, it's easier to *love* someone toward God's truth than to *argue* them there.

Humility always. Jesus saved His harshest words for religious people who believed in absolute truth and were trying to get everyone else to live by it. What was their problem? They were proud of themselves. The Pharisees' whole deal was showing that they were better than others. Maybe they were trying to be good examples, but it was all about *them.* Be willing to admit that you're not perfect, and that you have questions and doubts about truth. God's strength can shine through your weakness.

Live a life worth wanting. If you're a Christian, how does knowing the Truth Himself make your life better? What happiness does knowing Jesus bring you? Sometimes Christians seem like they're not having fun because . . . they aren't! This doesn't mean you should pretend that being a Christian is more fun than it is. It means asking God to help you develop the qualities He already wants to grow in you—like love, joy, and peace. It might help to hang out with a fun group of Christians, too.

Stay connected. Keep going back to God's Word and talking to Him in prayer. It's easy to twist the truth, even if we don't mean to. Staying connected to God and His Book helps keep us honest.

If you take a stand for God's truth, you *will* be misunderstood. Some people won't like what you have to say.

It takes courage. But it takes love, too.

After all, if we stop loving, we've missed the whole point of God's truth.

Twelve

FAQs

(Frequently Asked Questions)

When it comes to bottom-line truth, people have questions. Maybe you do, too. We'll get back to our chat room characters in a moment—but first, let's discuss some questions that may have popped into your mind as you've read this book.

Q. You can't totally prove there's a God, or that He's spoken "the truth" through the Bible or Christianity. The best you can say is that it's reasonable to believe these things. Well, it seems reasonable to me not to believe them. What do you say to that?

A. Lots of intelligent people have made that choice. But if you decide there's no God, then you have to answer three tough questions—about design, personality, and purpose.

First, you have to explain why the pieces of the universe fit together so well. If there's no Designer, how did this happen? Some would say that evolutionary processes caused this—in fact, some scientists talk about evolution almost as if it were a supreme being, having "infinite wisdom" and that sort of thing. But could chance mutations really create such an intricate world, such a complicated *you*?

Then you have to explain our personalities. Why do we laugh and cry? Why do we love? If there's no personal God who shared these bits of His personality with us, where did they come from? Chemicals? Some would say so. But are you willing to declare that true love is merely a chemical reaction, no more meaningful than the fizzing of vinegar and baking soda?

Then we come to the question of why we're here. If there's no Creator who made us to keep Him company, what purpose do we have? Maybe none—and a number of scientists and philosophers have reached that conclusion. But then why do we have such a strong *desire* for purpose in our lives? Where did that desire come from?

You're right—we can't totally prove the truth of Christianity. But each of us has a responsibility to weigh the evidence honestly.

As Biola University philosophy professor Dr. Doug Geivett points out, if we go by ordinary standards of reason and evidence, it makes sense to believe that God exists and the basic message of Christianity is true. Anyone who doesn't agree can try to show what's wrong with the evidence. The truth of Christianity may not be provable in the strictest sense, but that doesn't mean its reasonableness can't be demonstrated. The evidence may not be conclusive, but it's enough. Dr. Geivett concludes that it's reasonable to keep believing, at least until your evidence is defeated. And the evidence for Christianity hasn't been.

Q. I don't buy the "one truth fits all" idea. I think it's okay to do whatever you want as long as it doesn't hurt anybody. How could that be wrong?

A. It's good that you don't want to hurt anybody. That's

close to what Jesus said in the "Golden Rule"—"Do to others as you would have them do to you" (Luke 6:31). Nobody likes to get hurt, so don't hurt others.

"No hurting" isn't a bad rule. The problem is, we don't always know what hurts. And we aren't always honest about what we mean by hurting.

When people live by the Rule of Not Hurting, what are they really saying? Usually they're saying it's okay to cheat on a test because no one gets hurt. They're saying it's okay to lie to parents about where you're going at night, because no one gets hurt. They're saying it's okay to smoke dope, because who are you hurting? They're saying it's okay to have sex with any willing partner, because how will that affect anyone else?

So what they *really* mean is something like this:

"It's okay to do whatever you want as long as it doesn't hurt anybody . . . very much." When you cheat on a test, you're hurting others at least a little. It's like cutting in line. You gain an advantage by moving ahead, and everyone behind you is delayed a little. If you get better grades because you cheated, that puts you ahead of dozens of people who didn't cheat—and they fall back in class ranking or college acceptance because you cheated. This may seem picky—but if you're claiming to live by the Rule of Not Hurting, shouldn't you be consistent about it?

"It's okay to do whatever you want as long as it doesn't hurt anybody . . . right away." Having sex with your boyfriend or girlfriend might seem harmless right now. But what happens six months from now when you "fall out of love" with that person, and the breakup hurts even more because you've given yourselves to each other, body and soul? What happens in future relationships, when you feel cheap or

needy because of the sexual decisions you're making right now? If sex is intended as a precious gift from a wife to a husband and vice versa, you're also robbing both your future spouses of the full value of that gift.

"It's okay to do whatever you want as long as it doesn't hurt anybody . . . except yourself." If you get drunk or high on drugs, and don't hit someone with your car or rob convenience stores to support your habit, who are you hurting except yourself? Maybe no one. But don't belittle your own importance. Isn't your body worth taking care of? Aren't your thoughts worth thinking clearly?

"It's okay to do whatever you want as long as it doesn't hurt anybody . . . this time." Let's say you tell your parents you're going to the mall—but you and some friends go to a club instead, sneaking in with your fake IDs. You hear a great band and get home a bit late. "After the mall I went to Ty's house to watch TV," you lie. Your parents think you're the ideal kid, and you've had a great evening. No harm, no foul, right? But next time your driver might have a few drinks and get you all wrapped around a tree on the way home. Some of us love taking chances—and put ourselves and others in danger when we do.

"It's okay to do whatever you want as long as it doesn't hurt anybody . . . individually." So you get an extra five bucks back in change at the music store. Why not keep it? Who gets hurt? Just some corporate conglomerate. Plenty of adults cheat on their taxes for that reason, and some parents try to hide their money from college financial-aid offices. What's the harm in that? Maybe no individual gets hurt, but in a way everyone has to pay a tiny bit more for your cheating. And imagine your little brother or sister (if you have one) watching

you keep that extra five dollars. What does he or she learn? To grab as much money as possible, including any that might be lying around your room? Our example can hurt the people around us.

So if you live by the Rule of Not Hurting, be sure to apply it thoroughly. But don't stop there. Ask yourself, "What kind of person do I want to be? Is it enough merely to avoid hurting others, or do I want to help people, too? Do I want to be a trustworthy person? Do I want people to respect me for my integrity? What kind of life will I have if I always have to keep my lies straight? Wouldn't it be better to live by the truth?"

Q. Your "absolute" Christian truth changes all the time. You guys used to believe that women shouldn't go to school, slavery was okay, and racial segregation was great. How do I know your "unchanging" truth won't change again?

A. You had to bring that up! Yes, there are some viewpoints of yesteryear that Christians aren't proud of today. We've made some mistakes over the centuries. And sometimes we make the mistake of calling things "absolute" when they're just opinions or shifting interpretations of what God has said.

Strangely enough, though, past mistakes aren't a strong argument against the existence of absolute truth. According to Dr. Doug Geivett, it's right to adjust a belief when we discover it's mistaken. But that doesn't support the idea that there's no such thing as absolute truth. In fact, one who doesn't believe in absolute truth doesn't have much incentive to change a belief—even when evidence indicates it's mistaken.

Christians believe that God's truth is ultimate, unchanging, and must be applied to our lives. But it takes some interpretation to figure out how some of the truths God revealed to Moses and Paul fit with the modern lives of Brendan and Caitlin.

Still, the basics are clear. For example, the Bible plainly states that God made us; that human beings are sinful and need rescuing; that Jesus is the divine Son of God, sent to save us, and that He died on a cross and rose from the dead.

The Bible also teaches that the Spirit of God enters the lives of Christians and guides them "into all truth" (John 16:13). He helps us apply the Bible's teachings to our lives.

Our interpretations may change—because we make mistakes. But God's truth doesn't change—because He's already perfect.

Q. After I read a book like this, I feel fine about believing in ultimate truth. But when I get around my friends, I can't seem to remember any of the reasons why. What can I do?

A. Carry this book with you at all times!

Or not. If you're interested in sharing the message of this book, here are the highlights:

- We need ultimate meaning in our lives, but where will we find it?
- We can't have ultimate meaning unless we discover what's really true.
- In our search for truth, feelings are fickle. They can help sometimes, but they're often shallow.
- Public opinion is dangerous. Wise individuals can give us good advice, but crowds can easily lead us astray.
- Reasoning is helpful, but at some point we need God to reveal truth to us.

- God has revealed Himself in Jesus, who showed He was more than a great teacher and healer by rising from the dead—and in the Bible, the book that tells us about Him.

If you're looking for "killer" arguments to prove the resurrection of Christ, the creation of the universe, or the inspiration of the Bible, be careful. "Proving" will be tough, especially if people aren't ready to believe. And as Dr. Doug Geivett says, "Remember, nonbelievers take positions that they also should be prepared to support with good reasons. Christians should demonstrate their commitment to truth and acceptable standards of reason and evidence by listening sincerely to counterarguments. But they should not be expected to bear the whole burden of making sense of reality and offering good arguments for the sense they make."

You might want to reread sections of this book and review your own beliefs, but don't try to overwhelm people. Listen to their questions, let God's Spirit guide your answers, and respond with the knowledge you have. Never be afraid to say, "I don't know the answer, but I'll get back to you on that." Then do it.

Q. I believe in the Bible, but it doesn't tell me what's true in every situation—like what TV shows to watch, or how much to spend on clothes. How am I supposed to know the truth about these things?

A. The Bible gives us general guidelines about our priorities, attitudes, and actions. The Holy Spirit offers moment-to-moment help in applying those guidelines to our lives.

The Bible might not tell you exactly how much to spend on clothes, but it has plenty to say about the fact that God isn't as concerned with our outward appearance as He is with our hearts. It also tells us to be careful about the power of money and possessions, and the importance of using some of our money to care for the poor and to support God's work.

Does all of that give you a dollar amount? No. But it does give you some general guidelines, so when you're at the Gap pawing through the price tags you'll have a general idea about what to do.

The same pattern applies to TV shows and other entertainment. The Bible doesn't mention broadcast or cable; it talks about purity of heart, making good use of our time, and not totally removing ourselves from the world. In Philippians 4:8, we're told to focus our minds on whatever we find that's good or noble or true or excellent. That gives us some leeway, but also challenges us to pay attention to what goes into our brains.

God's truth is absolute in the biblical principles He gives us. But He allows some flexibility in how we work those out. Often there are several choices—buying this shirt or that one, skipping a new pair of shoes and putting the money in the offering plate or buying shoes and wearing them while you paint your elderly neighbor's house for free, etc.—that would equally please God.

Q. I'm not an atheist or anything. I just don't think it's possible to *know* whether there's really such a thing as absolute truth. If God is up there, why does He make it so hard for us to *know* these things? Why doesn't He make it obvious?

A. What do you want Him to do, raise someone from the dead? It could be argued that God *has* made it obvious, but many people don't want to believe it.

So think about it: What would you want God to do to help us know for sure? Would you want more miracles? But He's working miracles all the time. Nature itself is a miracle, and still people don't get it. Would you want Him to speak directly to our hearts, letting us know that He's there? Sometimes He does that, too—but He generally doesn't yell.

Maybe the problem is that the miracles aren't big enough, or radical enough. Maybe they're so commonplace that we easily ignore them. If He would only thunder from heaven and write in the sky, "I am God. Worship Me!" Then people would have to believe, wouldn't they? The sad fact is that most wouldn't—or they'd just build shrines and sell T-shirts to commemorate the event.

God has decided to work subtly, so that people who are ready to hear Him can hear Him. Maybe that's why Jesus sometimes said this after He taught: "He who has ears, let him hear" (Matthew 11:15).

Q. Okay, so you didn't make up the system that says Jesus is the only Way. But whoever made it up, it stinks. Can you honestly say it's fair that people who happen to have been brought up in another religion shouldn't get to go to heaven?

A. Maybe you're right. But God never promised to be fair, at least not by our definitions of fairness. Throughout the Bible, God announces that He has the right to do whatever He wants. He's God.

Yet the Bible also emphasizes His love. All of us deserve to be separated from God forever—since He's perfect and we're sinful—but He's lovingly made a way for us to know Him through His Son Jesus. If you want to talk fairness, consider that those who reject Jesus are getting what we *all* deserve.

But what about those who've never heard of Jesus? What

about those who grow up in religions that teach Jesus is their enemy? Shouldn't they get credit for being true to the religion they've learned?

The Bible says that God's existence is obvious in the universe He created, so that anyone can understand the basics of who God is. The Bible also indicates that those who seek a relationship with God can find it.

There's no question that, according to the Bible, Jesus Christ is the only Way to God. Yet there's a lot we don't know about how God speaks to human souls and how people respond to Him. Christians need to keep telling others the good news about Jesus, inviting people to God's eternal party—and let Him take care of the guest list.

Q. I have a good friend who belongs to a different religion. I want to keep him as a friend, not get in a big argument. Sure, I'd like it if he agreed with me about what's true, but what if he doesn't? Can't I just let it drop?

A. Yes. Don't stop caring about him, but drop the arguing. It's more likely that your relationship—not your arguments—will win him over. The Bible tells you to "Always be prepared to give an answer to everyone who asks you to give the reason for the hope that you have" (1 Peter 3:15). Be ready. Maybe your steel-trap mind can help sweep away one of your friend's questions at some point, but it's your love that will help attract him toward Jesus. That same verse urges Christians to speak to others "with gentleness and respect." Be sensitive to how God's Spirit is guiding you about when and how to talk about your faith.

Take some time to learn about your friend's religion. What elements of God's truth do you find there? Can you build a bridge from his beliefs to your belief in Jesus?

Check out what the Apostle Paul did while visiting Athens (Acts 17). Before speaking to the Athenians, he walked their streets to get a feel for what they believed. Then, instead of criticizing their multi-god religion, he used it to help them understand Christ. Paul had found a shrine "To an Unknown God"—the One they didn't know yet, the One Paul had come to tell them about.

Like the Athenians, people of many religions are reaching out to know what they can about the Creator. With love and sensitivity, you can help introduce them to Jesus.

WELCOME TO COLLEGE CHAT
Screen Name: jewel7
Logon 9:49 P.M.

	[College Chat welcomes new user jewel7.]
Iceman:	So, have you actually READ Nietzsche?
SOSO:	Read him? I can't even spell him!
Tim4U:	I prefer Kierkegaard.
Andee:	They're all so depressing.
jewel7:	tim, is that you?
Tim4U:	Yes, I'm Tim. Who are you?
jewel7:	it's julie. from the chat room
Tim4U:	What chat room?
Iceman:	She's stalking you in cyberspace.
SOSO:	Eerie.
jewel7:	that teentalk thing last year. i'm nobraner
Tim4U:	Yes! How are you?
jewel7:	good. in college now. syracuse
Tim4U:	Me, too. Not Syracuse. Taylor.

jewel7:	where's that?
Tim4U:	I'm still trying to figure that out. Somewhere in Indiana.
SOSO:	I'm at Notre Dame.
jewel7:	so what happened to you? you just left
Tim4U:	Sorry. I thought about coming back to the chat room, but . . .
jewel7:	they told me you got kinda flamed
SOSO:	Don't you hate that?
Andee:	I think they want to be alone.
Iceman:	Time to study anyway.
	[Goodbye to Iceman.]
SOSO:	I'll be quiet, I promise.
Tim4U:	To be honest, I got depressed about it all.
jewel7:	depression i know
Tim4U:	So whatever happened to everybody?
jewel7:	let's see . . . r2d2 won some science award, which he dedicated to his teacher
Tim4U:	Of course.
jewel7:	hulkster got in trouble. he was cut from the football team so he went out and demolished like five cars
Tim4U:	With his bare hands.
jewel7:	yep
Tim4U:	Kinda makes me glad I only knew him on the Net.
jewel7:	who else do you want to know about?
Tim4U:	Butterfly. Did she ever get back with Jared, or that other guy?
jewel7:	nope. she started seeing a new guy, but it got too physical for her so she ended it
Tim4U:	Never seems to get easier for her, does it?

jewel7:	she e-mails me once in a while. what should i tell her about you?
Tim4U:	That I burned out on the chat room, I guess. I mean, I was trying to do the right thing, but no one was listening.
jewel7:	i was
Tim4U:	Thanks, but it's just so frustrating. Doesn't anyone care about truth anymore?
jewel7:	i care
Tim4U:	Thanks . . . again.
jewel7:	i should be thanking you. you dared to ask me tough questions. you introduced me to jesus
Tim4U:	I did?
jewel7:	i thought you knew that. i'm a christian now because of you. i'm probably ALIVE now because of you
Tim4U:	Wow!
jewel7:	so thank YOU
SOSO:	This is so beautiful!
Andee:	Ssssshhhhhhhh!
jewel7:	but i do have more questions for you
Tim4U:	How about tomorrow night? I've got to hit the books.
jewel7:	okay. see you then, virtually speaking
Tim4U:	I'll be here.

Smiling, Julie clicked her laptop computer shut and moved it to a corner of her dorm room desk.

She reached to the bookshelf above her, pulling down a red leather-bound Bible. She opened it to the place marked by a scarlet ribbon, and, once more, began to read.

For Further Reading

Want to read more about the whys and hows of believing, living, and sharing ultimate truth? Here are some books you might try:

Answers to Tough Questions Skeptics Ask about the Christian Faith by Josh McDowell and Don Stewart (Tyndale House, 1986)

Christianity: Hoax or History? (Pocket Guide) by Josh McDowell (Tyndale House, 1989)

Don't Check Your Brains at the Door by Josh McDowell and Bob Hostetler (Word Books, 1992)

Evidence That Demands a Verdict: Historical Evidences for the Christian Faith by Josh McDowell (Volume 1) (Thomas Nelson, 1999)

How to Stay Christian in College: An Interactive Guide to Keeping the Faith by J. Budziszewski (NavPress, 1999)

Keeping Your Cool While Sharing Your Faith by Greg Johnson and Susie Shellenberger (Tyndale House, 1993)

Know What You Believe by Paul E. Little (ChariotVictor, 1999)

Know Why You Believe by Paul E. Little (Intervarsity Press, 2000)

More Than a Carpenter by Josh McDowell (Tyndale House, 1987)

Right from Wrong by Josh McDowell and Bob Hostetler (Word Books, 1994)

True for You, but Not for Me: Deflating the Slogans That Leave Christians Speechless by Paul Copan (Bethany House, 1998)

What High School Students Should Know about Evolution by Kenneth Taylor (Tyndale House, 1983)

Who Should I Listen To? by Kevin Johnson (Bethany House, 1993)

Up to more challenging reading? You might try these books:

Baker Encyclopedia of Christian Apologetics by Norman L. Geisler (Baker Book House, 1999)

Darwin on Trial by Phillip E. Johnson (Intervarsity Press, 1993)

How Now Shall We Live? by Charles Colson and Nancy Pearcey (Tyndale House, 1999)

Mere Christianity by C.S. Lewis (Broadman and Holman, 2000)

The Creation Hypothesis: Scientific Evidence for an Intelligent Designer, J.P. Moreland, editor (Intervarsity Press, 1994)

The God Who Is There by Francis Schaeffer and James W. Sire (Intervarsity Press, 1998)

(Note: Though the preceding books contain helpful information, not all the views expressed in all of them are necessarily endorsed by Focus on the Family.)

ABOUT THE AUTHOR

Randy Petersen is a free-lance writer who lives in New Jersey. He has 30 books to his credit, including *The Family Book of Bible Fun* (Tyndale) and *Charge It on the Master's Card* (Revell). He also writes youth curriculum, directs high school plays as well as productions at other theaters, and teaches acting. At his church Randy helps lead the singles group, teaches, sometimes preaches, sings, directs the drama group, and plays third base on the softball team.

Are You Ready to Live Life on the Edge?

At Focus on the Family, we are committed to helping you learn more about Jesus Christ and preparing you to change your world for Him! We realize the struggles you face are different from your mom's or your little brother's, so Focus on the Family has developed a ton of stuff specifically for you! They'll get you ready to boldly live out your faith no matter what situation you find yourself in.

We don't want to tell you what to do. We want to encourage and equip you to be all God has called you to be in every aspect of life! That may involve strengthening your relationship with God, solidifying your values and perhaps making some serious changes in your heart and mind.

We'd like to come alongside you as you consider God's role in your life, discover His plan for you in the lives of others and how you can impact your generation to change the world.

We have conferences, Web sites, magazines, palm-sized topical booklets, fiction books, a live call-in radio show . . . all dealing with the topics and issues that *you* deal with and care about. For a more complete and detailed listing of what we have available for you, visit our Web site at www.family.org. Then click on "Resources," followed by either "Teen Girls" or "Teen Guys."

• • •

Trying to reach us?

In the United States:

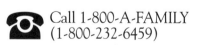

Focus on the Family
Colorado Springs, CO
80995

Call 1-800-A-FAMILY
(1-800-232-6459)

In Canada:

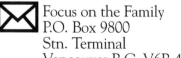

Focus on the Family
P.O. Box 9800
Stn. Terminal
Vancouver B.C. V6B 4G3

Call 1-800-661-9800

To find out if there is an associate office in your country visit www.family.org.

Visit our Web site:
www.family.org

We'd love to hear from you!